Tackling Computer Projects

in Access with Visual Basic for Applications

4th edition

P.M. Heathcote

B.Sc.(Hons), M.Sc.

Payne-Gallway Publishers Ltd
26-28 Northgate Street
Ipswich
IP1 3DB
Tel: 01473-251097 Fax: 01473 232758
E-mail: info@payne-gallway.co.uk
Web site: http//www.payne-gallway.co.uk

2004

Acknowledgements

I would like to thank:

The Assessment and Qualifications Alliance for permission to use the scenario *Tod's Tyres*;

Alison Day for providing a sample solution to *Tod's Tyres*, instructions on how to implement it and many useful tips for students;

Helen Williams for providing the 'Moderator's Comments' to the sample project in Part 3 of the fourth edition and making valuable comments and suggestions;

Matthew Strawbridge for updating Parts 2 and 3 to the latest version of MS Access;

My daughter Flora who did much of the original work of developing the application described in Parts 2 and 3 of this book for a local business. Six years later, the original application is still running error-free and being used by the business on a daily basis.

A CIP catalogue entry for this book is available from the British Library

ISBN 1 904467 53 9

Copyright PM Heathcote © 2004

First edition 1992. Reprinted 1993, 1996

Second edition 1997. Reprinted 1998, 1999

Third edition 2000. Reprinted 2001, 2002, 2003

Fourth edition 2004.

Printed in Great Britain by
W M Print Ltd
45-47 Frederick Street
Walsall, West Midlands

Foreword

Pat Heathcote's books provide many students, their lecturers and teachers with clear, concise information on a wide range of computing topics. Students find her books easy to use for initial learning and as a revision aid.

'Tackling Computer Projects' has become a standard text for students providing an indispensable guide to the development of their project work. The book gives an insight into the tasks and structure required to develop a successful Computing Project.

The fourth edition has been revised to reflect new examination board marking requirements. Once again, this book is very easy to read and would be an invaluable guide to anyone developing a Computing Project. As many students now choose to use MS Access and Visual Basic as their software development tools, chapters twelve to eighteen will be particularly helpful in aiding their production of a really professional computerised system.

Students following the advice and guidance provided in this book should be able to produce a project report that meets examination board guide-lines and also develop a real, useable software solution.

Helen Williams
Principal Moderator and Examiner
September 2004

Preface

The fourth edition

The fourth edition includes a brand new Part 1, aimed at helping 'AS' Level students complete a database project or task. Part 2 will help 'A2' students to select a suitable project and go through the stages of analysis, design, implementation, testing and documentation. It will also serve as a useful introduction to programming in Visual Basic for Applications. Some specifications such as the AQA 'A' Level Computing require extensive customisation in a programming language, and the sample project will give students an idea of how this can be approached. However, following the given examples slavishly will not produce a top grade and students *must* find their own ways of fulfilling the requirements of a real user.

Aim

The aim of this book is to provide students with a comprehensive and practical guide on how to tackle a computing project for an Advanced Level Computing or Information Technology course. It will also be useful to students doing a project for a GCSE or Higher National computing course, since the principles remain the same at any level.

Approach

This book is suitable for students either on a taught course or studying independently, as it can be used with no additional help from a lecturer.

Part 1 of the book shows how to develop and test a simple database, using as an example *Tod's Tyres*, the task set by AQA in 2004.

Part 2 follows through all the steps involved in completing a project using MS Access 2003. Instructions for earlier versions of Access are included where necessary.

Part 3 shows the final project developed from the prototype to a finished solution satisfying all the objectives set out by the user. Comments from a moderator are included: grading will depend on the particular assessment criteria being used.

Lecturers' supplement

The database solutions for the sample projects in Parts 1 and 3 are available free to lecturers from our web site www.payne-gallway.co.uk

Part 1

Introducing Access

In this section:

Chapter 1 – The Scenario: Tod's Tyres

Objectives

By the end of this chapter you should have:

Read through the scenario for the set task and established the objectives of the proposed system;

Worked out the data requirements, i.e. the data that needs to be entered in order to produce the desired output;

Understood the meaning of the terms **entity**, **attribute**, **relationship** and **primary key**.

What is a database?

Most people have some idea that databases are used to store data but beyond that, the details are a little hazy. The easiest way of learning more about what constitutes a database is to actually create one, so you will learn more about databases as you learn about the features of MS Access. This is a practical book about how to use Access, but it will also guide you through the various stages of developing a project – including analysis, design, implementation, testing and documentation. It is primarily aimed at students on a Computing course, so Part 2 will involve quite a lot of programming in Visual Basic for Applications to customise the solution to the user's requirements.

Introduction to the scenario

Part 1 of the book will take you through the process of designing and implementing a simple database for a sample application called **Tod's Tyres**. This scenario was used in the AQA Practical Exercise for Module 3 of 'AS' Level Computing in 2004, and will be a useful introduction to MS Access whether or not you are following this course.

Before you can start to design any database, there are some questions that need to be answered.

- What is this database for?
- What tasks should it do?
- What output is required?
- What data needs to be put into the database in order to get the required output?
- What format should each data item be in? Is it text, numeric (integer or real), currency or date/time?
- What processing needs to be carried out on the data – will any calculations be needed?

The scenario is described below. Read it carefully and make some notes, which will help you to understand what is required and how it can be achieved. You should be able to answer most of the above questions after you have read the scenario.

Background

Tod's Tyres is a small business which supplies new tyres to company car fleets and car hire firms.

You have been asked to create a computer application, **either programmed or using a database,** to replace the current manual record-keeping system. Initially, at least, there will be only one standalone workstation with a printer attached. This is to be kept locked in the office.

For the purposes of this exercise, you may assume that all the cars have the post-2001 format car registration number, e.g. AB 03 XYZ.

Current system

1. When a car is brought to Tod for the first time, the following information is recorded on a card: car registration number, company name, type of tyre fitted. Each time that the car has new tyres the date, car mileage, and number of new tyres fitted is recorded on the card. There is also space to make a comment; for example, the mechanic fitting the tyres may have noted some other problem with the car, which they would bring to the notice of the customer so that it could be sorted out. When a card becomes full, a new card is stapled to the original one. These cards are filed in car registration number order.

2. The next time the company books in a recorded car for new tyres, Tod checks the card file to see what type of tyre that car has fitted. He then ensures that he has the required tyres in stock. He prides himself that he never lets a regular customer down.

3. Tod gets his tyres from one supplier only. This supplier sends him an up-to-date supplier price list once a month. Todd then adds his fitting costs to produce a customer price list. The current price list is as follows.

Type	Manufacturer's Code	Customers' Price (Ex VAT)
155/80S13	P1000	£36.00
165/80S13	P3000	£39.00
155/80S14	P5000	£58.50
165/80S14	P7000	£64.00

4. Some companies are allowed a 5% discount before VAT is added. At present, Tod does not keep a record of who these are because he can remember them. However, a computerised system would have to keep a record.

5. VAT is payable at the current rate.

6. Tod keeps company details (company name, contact name, address, post code and telephone number) in another card file.

7. Tod supplies an invoice to his customers. This invoice is supplied in duplicate, one copy for the customer and one for Tod's own record for his accountant. It has an invoice number in the top right hand corner. It details the date, company name, postcode and telephone number, car registration number, number of tyres supplied with their price, discount where applicable and VAT.

8. Once a month, one of the clerks goes through the cards and pulls out cards for cars which last had new tyres over a year ago and so might be ready for new tyres. Tod then sends the customer a standard letter reminding them that the tyres are ready for replacement, and quoting them a price.

9. Tod also intends to use a popular word processing package. He wants to use the Internet and e-mail in the near future, and possibly have his own Web site. He feels that a move into electronic communication would be beneficial to his business. You should bear these plans in mind when designing your system, although you are not expected to incorporate these applications for this exercise.

Testing

Car registration numbers should be validated and the number of tyres sold for one vehicle at any one time should not exceed 5. Testing should ensure that the calculations produce the correct result.

Requirements of the practical exercise

If you are following Unit 3 of the AQA 'A' Level Computing course, you will be given the following instructions.

Candidates will need to design and implement an appropriate computing system and provide sufficient documentation to demonstrate the following practical skills:

- Design
- Implement/Test.

For the purpose of this exercise, the actual implementation of the sending of the standard letter to customers is not required, although thought should be given as to how this would be implemented.

The task may be undertaken by:

either writing a program in a chosen high-level language

or using a suitable application package.

Candidates are expected to produce brief documentation including some or all of the following, as appropriate.

Design

- Definition of data requirements
- User interface design including output, forms and reports
- Method of data entry, including validation
- Record structure, file organisation and processing
- Security and integrity of data
- System design

Implementation/Testing

- Details of test plan with explanation, and evidence of testing having been carried out
- Hard copy output of the invoice, with and without discount
- Hard copy of solution e.g. annotated program listing/database tables, forms and reports.

We will take the **Analysis** of the problem as described in the Brief, and concentrate entirely on the **Design** and **Implementation and Testing** of a solution to this practical exercise. Note that there is no unique 'correct' solution, although there are some 'wrong' approaches. The problem could be solved in a variety of ways, such as by writing a program, by using a database application package, or by a combination of these. In this book, we are looking at a database approach.

The given solution will be used to introduce some Access features which could prove useful when tackling a similar task.

Objectives

When given a problem or scenario such as Tod's Tyres, the first thing to do is to establish the **objectives** of the required system. You should already have written down some answers to the questions:

What is this database for? What tasks should it do? What output is required?

Your list of answers for what Tod wants his database to enable him to do should look something like this:

1.   Enter details of a new company
2.   Enter details of a new car
3.   Book a tyre fitting
4.   Check that the right tyre is in stock
5.   Enter a comment, if necessary, as a result of a fitting
6.   Produce an invoice (in duplicate)
7.   Produce a reminder letter to customers (although you do not actually have to produce this for this exercise)
8.   Update the tyre price list.

Data requirements

The data items required for each of the above are:

1.	Enter details of a new company	Company name, address & telephone number, contact name
2.	Enter details of cars	Registration number, tyre type
3.	Enter details of a tyre fitting	Registration number, mileage, fitting date, number of tyres required
4.	Check that the right tyre is in stock	Tyre type, number in stock, number required
5.	Enter a comment, if necessary, as a result of a fitting	Registration number, date, comment
6.	Produce an invoice (in duplicate).	Invoice number, company name & address, date of fitting, car registration number, number of tyres fitted, customer price, discount (if any), VAT
7.	Produce a reminder letter to customers	Car registration number, date of last fitting, tyre type, customer price, discount (if any), VAT
8.	Update tyre price list	Tyre type, manufacturer's code, cost price, customer price

Entities, attributes and tables

In database terminology, a person or thing of interest to an organisation, about which data is stored, is called an **entity**. For example, an entity could be a customer, a tyre or an invoice. Each entity in a database has **attributes** which tell us something about the entity: for example a customer has attributes **name**, **address** and **telephone number**.

The first step in creating your database is to design and create the structures that will store the data. In Access, data is stored in **Tables**; one table for each entity. You need to decide:

- what entities are needed. Then for each entity,
  - its attributes
  - the data type and format of each attribute.

You also need to choose which attribute or attributes will be the **primary key field** for each entity. The primary key field will a field such as **company ID** or **car registration number** that uniquely identifies a particular row or record in a table.

Tod's old manual system had three different card files:

- car records

- company details

- details of tyres and their prices.

COMPANY and **TYRE** will neatly transfer to two entities in the database, although you may need to update these slightly.

Relationships between entities

Tod's original **CAR** card file stored the fixed details of the cars, such as registration number, company name, and type of tyre fitted as well as the variable details, such as how many tyres were fitted and when, and comments that the fitters made. If you tried to put these into one table, how would you know how many fittings to leave room for? Too many would be cumbersome and a waste of space. Too few would cause a problem when you needed an extra fitting.

One solution is to have two tables: one called **CAR**, to store the unchanging details and the other called **FITTING**, to store each fitting. The tables will be linked by the car registration number. The relationship between the two entities is simple:

Figure 1.1: Entity-relationship diagram

The relationships between the four entities can be expressed as:

ONE company has MANY cars

ONE car has MANY fittings

MANY cars have ONE tyre type

Here is a complete entity relationship diagram for the four entities you will set up:

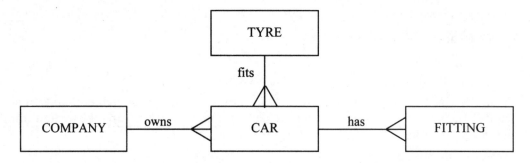

Figure 1.2: Entity Relationship diagram

Chapter 2 – Database Design

Objectives

By the end of this chapter you should have:

designed the tables, forms and reports needed for the database;

designed a test plan and made up suitable test data.

In Chapter 1 the scenario was introduced and the data requirements were decided upon. We decided that four related entities were involved: **Company**, **Car**, **Tyre** and **Fitting**.

The next stage is to design all the tables, input forms, queries and reports you will need to satisfy all the objectives. You need to decide what validations will be performed, and what the input forms and reports will look like. For this, you are well-advised to use paper and pencil before loading Access.

We will start by designing the four tables, which involves deciding what fields need to go in each table and what data type, etc., they will be. Because you are probably just learning to use Access as you work through this book, you may find that the best way of learning is to read quickly through this chapter and proceed to Chapter 3. You can keep referring back to this chapter to understand *why* you are implementing the database in the manner shown.

Data type and format

At this stage you must decide on the data type and format of each attribute. Access has a selection of different data types, including these:

Data type	Comment
Text	Text, or a mixture of text and numbers, or numbers that do not require calculations. Up to 255 characters in length.
Memo	Up to 65535 characters
Number	Either Integer (Byte, Integer or Long Integer) or Real (Single or Double)
Date/Time	Various formats are available
Currency	For monetary values

*An **integer** is a whole number; a **real number** has decimal places.*

Table 2.1

Attribute names in Access can be as long as you like, and can contain spaces and other characters. We will use names with no spaces, using 'CamelCaps', i.e. capitalising each new word in the name to make them stand out and be easier to read.

Naming conventions

There are various conventions for naming objects in Access. You don't have to use a naming convention but doing so will make the database easier to use and, more importantly, to maintain. This book uses the Leszynski/Reddick naming conventions, a sample of which are shown in Table 2.2:

Object	Tag	Example
Table	tbl	tblTyre
Query	qry	qryInvoice
Form	frm	frmCar
Report	rpt	rptInvoice

Table 2.2

Designing the tables

For each table, you must specify the **Field name**, **Data type**, **Field length** or **format** and **Validation rule** or **input mask**. You can add comments where appropriate.

Validation rules and masks will be discussed in Chapter 4. Field lengths have been chosen to be sensible, but the final choice is up to you.

tblTyre

Field name	Data type	Field length / format	Comments / Description	Validation rule / input mask
TyreType	Text	9	Primary key	
ManufacturersCode	Text	5	The tyre code assigned by the manufacturer	
SupplierPrice	Currency	default	From the supplier price list	
CustomerPrice	Currency	default	Tyre price charged to customer, excluding VAT	
NumberInStock	Number	byte		

Table 2.3

In this case, because the system has been simplified from real life, there are two unique fields, (**TyreType** and **ManufacturersCode**) and you have a choice of primary key. In real life, a garage would probably use more than one manufacturer, as customers would have different preferences. The tyre type refers to factors such as tyre diameter and width. In this exercise, **TyreType** is chosen as the primary key.

tblCompany

Field Name	Data Type	Length/ Format	Comments/ Description	Validation rule / input mask
CompanyID	Text	5	Primary Key	>LLL00 *(explained in Chapter 4)*
CompanyName	Text	30		
ContactTitle	Text	5	Mr, Mrs etc.	
ContactInitial	Text	1		
ContactSurname	Text	20		
AddressLine1	Text	25	Name/Number and Street	
AddressLine2	Text	25	Town	
PostCode	Text	8		
TelephoneNumber	Text	11		
Discount	Yes/No			

Table 2.4

CompanyID has been added to serve as the primary key instead of **CompanyName**. Tod may well service different branches of the same company, and it is sensible to have a short code to uniquely identify each customer. The field lengths allocated to names and addresses are your choice. You could look in a telephone directory to get some idea of what is appropriate.

You also need to specify whether or not a company gets a discount. One of the data types available in Access is **Yes/No**, which is ideal for this purpose.

Whenever you are designing an application involving any kind of mail merge, you need to store title, initial and surname separately. This is so that at the top of the letter you can have a name like **Mr. J. Matthews** and in the salutation line you can have **Dear Mr Matthews** and not **Dear Mr J. Matthews** which is incorrect.

Choose **Text** for **TelephoneNumber** because you will not be doing any calculations on this field. If you choose a **Number** data type, the leading zero will be dropped and you will not be able to insert spaces in the phone number.

tblCar

Field name	Data type	Length / Format	Comments / Description	Validation rule / input mask
RegistrationNumber	Text	7	Primary Key	>LL00LLL *(see Chapter 4)*
CompanyID	Text	5	Foreign key, looked up from tblCompany	
TyreType	Text	9	Foreign key, looked up from tblTyre	
DateOfLastFitting	Date/Time	Medium Date		

Table 2.5

tblFitting

Attribute	Data Type	Length / Format	Comments / Description	Validation rule / input mask
RegistrationNumber	Text	7	Primary Key	>LL00LLL *(see Chapter 4)*
FittingDate	Date / Time	Medium Date	Primary Key	
NumberOfTyres	Number	Byte		Between 1 and 5 Or Is Null
Mileage	Number	Long Integer	Could be useful to answer customer complaints etc.	
Comment	Memo			
InvoiceNumber	AutoNumber		Unique, no duplicates	

Table 2.6

The field **Mileage** may be held for possible future requirements, and is one of the data items currently stored in Tod's manual system.

You need to consider how you will be able to find when a car was last fitted with one or more new tyres. We will have a field called **DateOfLastFitting** on **tblCar**, and when a car comes in for a fitting, Tod will need to update that field. Alternatively, when you become expert at using Visual Basic for Applications, you could write code to update the field automatically when **FittingDate** is entered in **tblFitting**.

Once you are more expert in Access and understand more about its capabilities, you will be able to design the tables, forms, queries and reports that you need for your own project. In the meantime, you may prefer to go straight to Chapter 3 and get some valuable practical experience.

Processing design

'Processing' includes any formulae you need in order to calculate, for example, VAT, discount and the total amount at the bottom of the invoice for a tyre fitting. It also includes designing the queries that will sort data, select records obeying particular conditions (criteria) and combine fields from several tables.

Think about the calculations that are required for the Tod's Tyres scenario.

For the invoice:

CostBeforeDiscount = NumberOfTyres * CustomerPrice

Discount = CostBeforeDiscount * DiscountRate (if discount is to be applied to this customer)

NetCost = CostBeforeDiscount – Discount

VAT = NetCost * VAT Rate

TotalCost = NetCost + VAT

These calculations will be done in a query **qryInvoice**.

For the reminder letters:

Find all the cars where the latest fitting was over a year ago. This will be done by means of a query **qryReminder** which will combine data from **tblFitting**, **tblCar** and **tblCompany**.

The query could use the criterion

DateOfLastFitting>=date()-365   (i.e. today's date -365)

The problem is that customers who don't respond to the letter will get a letter once a month for the rest of their lives until they do … so you could think about that problem!

Perhaps a better criterion would be

FittingDate Between Date()-350 And Date()-380

This allows for the fact that it will take a few days to get the letters out and probably a few days for the customer to book in for a fitting.

Form design

All data entry will be done using on-screen forms, and you can also have a menu form which will be displayed automatically when the database opens. This allows the user to select what they want to do, such as enter details of a fitting or print an invoice.

Four forms are needed for Tod to carry out his tasks:

1.   **frmCompany** – for details of each company

2.   **frmCar** – for details of each car

3.   **frmFitting** – to book a fitting, check there are sufficient tyres in stock, record any comment as a result of the fitting and update the 'Date of last fitting' field for the reminder letter

4.   **frmTyre** – to update customer price list

In addition, a menu called a **switchboard**, from which any task can be selected, will be added as a front end.

Reports

The only report that needs to be produced is the invoice. You should look at a sample of invoices to see how the information is generally laid out, and produce a design.

You should also think about exactly what fields will be needed on the reminder letter – it would be worth producing a hand-written draft. The final letter might look something like this:

Tod's Tyres

Mrs B Jones
Express Hire
Station
Cambertown
GU135GH

16/07/2004

Dear Mrs Jones

Ref: SL53OGH

According to our records, you last had new tyres fitted to this car on 02/07/2003.
Our records show that this car needs tyres of type: 165/80S14
If the vehicle now needs new tyres, we would like to quote you the following price per tyre:

Cost price:	£64.00
Discount @ 5%:	£3.20
Net cost	£60.80
VAT @ 17.5%	£10.64
Total Price	£71.44

Please call us on 01234 567567 to make an appointment. Assuring you of our best attention at all times.

Yours sincerely,

For S Tod (Proprietor)

Figure 2.1

Testing

You should plan how you are going to test your application, and include test data and a test plan in the design documentation. You need to test the following:

- All validations work correctly
- All forms are easy to use and contain all fields in the correct order so that the user can tab through them
- All calculations are correctly performed
- All reports contain all the required information and are laid out correctly in an easy-to-read format.

When making up test data you need to include erroneous data to test your validations, and data on the boundaries of what is acceptable to make sure that validations are fully correct. For example, if the number of tyres should be between 1 and 5 you could include test data with 0, 1, 3, 5 and 6 tyres.

Here is a test plan and some test data. We will be using this test data to make sure that the system works correctly.

Test plan

Construct a test plan, built around the list of things to be tested.. You do not need to provide evidence of every test, but you should produce evidence of a representative selection. Also, where a point has been specifically made in the brief, for example, car registration number should be validated and the number of tyres should not exceed 5, these matters should be tested and you should produce evidence of that testing.

Test No.	Testing	Data	Form / Query / Report	Expected Result
1	Registering new customer	Mr M Gower WES01 West Heath Service Engineers 221 Gordon Rd West Heath GU217BH 01932354857	frmCompany	Entered in Customer table
2	Registering new car	GU03WIN West Heath SE 155/80S13	frmCar	Selected Payne Cars; Mr O Heath displayed. New car entered in Car table
3	Registering new car where customer not registered	IQ53NYR HandyCars	frmCar	Unable to enter HandyCars, and so new car not accepted
4	Invalid registration number	RQ1DNG	frmCar	Unable to enter D without second digit

5	Booking car in for fitting	GU03WIN WES01 165/80S14 16/07/04 4 tyres	frmFitting	Selected car registration; Company name and contact displayed No. in Stock displayed
6	Booking new car in for fitting where car not registered	IQ53NYR HandyCars	frmFitting	Car not found; unable to book fitting
7	Maximum no. of tyres Extreme value	SL53OGH 25/01/03 5 tyres	frmFitting	OK
8	Erroneous data	GN02QER 21/01/03 A tyres	frmFitting	Error message. Not allowed to carry on until error corrected.
9	Too many tyres Boundary value	GU03WIN 16/07/04 6 tyres	frmFitting	Error message. Not allowed to carry on until error corrected
10	Finding record to add comment	GU03WIN	frmFitting	Use Find for desired record
11	Adding comment to fitting	GU03WIN 'MOT expired last week'	frmFitting	Comment accepted
12	Looking for a car which had not had a recent fitting		frmFitting	'Find' drew a blank
13	Invoice calculation correct	GU03WIN 16/07/04 (no discount)	rptInvoice	Calculation correct
14	Invoice calculation correct	GU02UGH 14/07/04 discount	rptInvoice	calculation correct
15	Reminder letter – correct selection	Between 16/07/04 – 350 and 16/07/04 – 380 days	qryReminder	Selection correct
16	Reminder letter – correct selection	Before 12 ½ months ago or later than 11 ½ months ago or not last fitting	qryReminder	Fitting not selected
17	Reminder letter without discount		rptReminder	calculation correct
18	Reminder letter with discount		rptReminder	calculation correct

Table 2.7

Test data

The following test data will be used:

Company Test Data

tblCompany

Compa nyID	Company Name	Contact Name	Address1	Address2	PostCode	Telephone Number	Disc ount
EUR01	EuroHire	Mr B Patten	42, Industrial Way	Dean	GU12OLD	01267645345	Yes
EXP01	Express Hire	Mrs B Jones	Station Approach	Cambertown	GU135GH	01267377377	No
MAK01	MakeWay Motors	Mr J Pierce	37 Thatchem Rd	Catford	RG213RB	01183672345	Yes
MAS01	Masterson Taxis	Ms B Masters	112, New Road	Sunningfield	RG124GH	01181236576	Yes
PAY01	Payne Cars	Mr O Heath	12 Old St	Bramley	GU243SW	01234567812	No
WES01	West Heath Service Engineers	Mr M Gower	221, Gordon Rd	West Heath	GU217BH	01932354857	No

Table 2.8

Car Test Data

tblCar

RegistrationNumber	CompanyID	TyreType	DateOfLastFitting
BR02SWI	PAY01	165/80S14	11-Jun-04
BR03DEV	PAY01	155/80S14	02-Aug-03
GN02UGH	EUR01	155/80S13	14-Jul-04
GN03YES	EUR01	165/80S13	09-Aug-03
GR04FLK	EUR01	165/80S14	02-Jul-04
GU03WIN	WES01	155/80S13	16-Jul-04
GX03DEX	EUR01	155/80S13	07-May-04
RG03FRD	MAS01	155/80S13	05-Oct-03
RG03NOW	MAK01	155/80S13	11-Jun-04
RG51DDL	MAS01	155/80S14	01-Jul-03
RG52SWE	MAS01	155/80S13	01-Aug-03
RG53ABC	MAK01	165/80S13	07-Jan-04
RG53NPW	MAK01	165/80S14	05-Dec-03
SL52OUG	EXP01	155/80S14	10-Jul-03
SL53OGH	EXP01	165/80S14	02-Jul-03

Table 2.9

Tyre Test Data

tblTyre

TyreType	Manufacturers Code	CostPrice	CustomerPrice	NumberIn Stock
155/80S13	P1000	£25.00	£36.00	17
165/80S13	P3000	£30.00	£39.00	14
155/80S14	P5000	£44.50	£58.50	21
165/80S14	P7000	£49.00	£64.00	11

Table 2.10

Fitting Test Data

tblFitting

Registration Number	Date	Number OfTyres	Mileage	Comment	Invoice Number
GN02UGH	12-Jan-03	2	458620		1
BR02SWI	12-May-03	2	35785		4
RG51DDL	01-Jul-03	2	64213		5
SL53OGH	02-Jul-03	3	39524		6
GN02UGH	11-Jul-03	4	69524		7
RG52SWE	01-Aug-03	1	76241		8
BR03DEV	02-Aug-03	3	38210		9
GX03DEX	07-May-04	3	37241		10
RG03NOW	11-Jun-04	4	45860		11
BR02SWI	11-Jun-04	3	78956		12
GN02UGH	14-Jul-04	3	0	Hand break tightened	13
GU03WIN	16-Jul-04	4	56784	MOT expired last week	14

Table 2.11

Chapter 3 – Introducing Access

Objectives

By the end of this chapter you should have:
created and linked the tables needed for the database.

We are ready to start implementing the table designs from the previous chapter. Before you load up Access and start creating your database, you should create a new folder in a suitable location. You could name this folder, for example, **TodsDatabase**.

Create a blank database in Access

- Open Access, either by double clicking on the key icon, or via **Start, Programs, Microsoft Access**.

- Select **Create a new File...**

- Select **Blank database...**

- Choose a suitable folder (e.g. **TodsDatabase**) in which to save your database.

- Type the file name **Tod** and click on **Create**.

Tip:
*If you leave the name at the default **db1** then you run the risk of overwriting it when you next create a new database – and will have to re-do all your hard work!*

The Access Database window

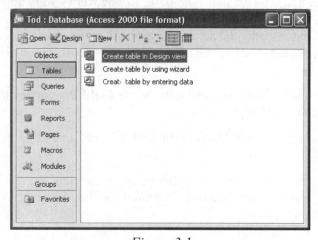

Figure 3.1

The first thing to note is that a database is made up of a number of items including:

- ◆ Tables   for storing data, as has already been mentioned
- ◆ Queries   for searching and extracting data
- ◆ Forms   for inputting and examining data
- ◆ Reports   for presenting the output from those queries in hard copy
- ◆ Macros and modules   for customizing the database and the way it is used

Table design view

We will start by creating the tyre table, **tblTyre**. The fields needed in this table are described in Table 2.3 in Chapter 2.

- Double-click **Create Table in Design View**. You will be offered a blank table.

- Enter the first tyre attribute name (field name), **TyreType**, and press the **Tab** key. **Text** is the default **Data Type**, so leave it.

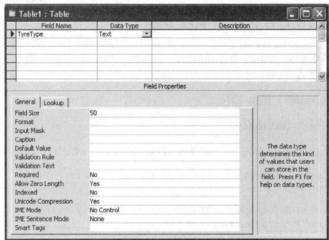

Figure 3.2

The default field length for **Text** data type is 50. If you were setting up a really large database, leaving a small field on 50 could waste space – although ever since Version 1.0, Access has been intelligent enough to store only the actual characters that you enter into each text field. Other database packages are not so clever, so declaring a realistic maximum size for each text field is a good habit to get into.

- Move your cursor down to **Field Size** in the **Field Properties** in the bottom part of the screen and change *50* to *9*.

- Enter the next field name **ManufacturersCode** and amend its field size to *5* in the same way.

- Enter the next field name, **SupplierPrice**, then click on the arrowhead, and select **Currency** (Figure 3.3). The default format for this data type is two decimal places, as required.

Field Name	Data Type	Description
TyreType	Text	
ManufacturersCode	Text	
▶ CostPrice	Currency	Ex VAT

Figure 3.3

- Add a note in the description column for this field: '**Ex VAT**'.

- Enter the next field name, **CustomerPrice**, and select **Currency**. Add a note in the description column for this field: '**Ex VAT**'.

- Enter the final field name **NumberInStock**, and select the **Number** data type. Leave it on the default **Long Integer**.

Setting a primary key field

- To set **TyreType** as the primary key, select that row and then click on the **Primary Key** icon in the toolbar.

- Select **File**, **Save** to save the table. Name it **tblTyre**. (Alternatively, you can click on the **X** to close it and save it when asked in the dialogue box.)

Your finished table will look like Figure 3.4.

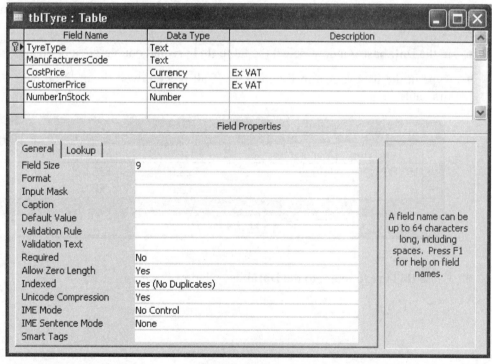

Figure 3.4

Warning

If you have forgotten to set **TyreType** as the primary key, you will get this dialogue box.

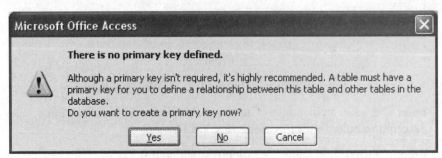

Figure 3.5

- Click **Cancel** and go back and set **TyreType** to be the primary key as suggested.

Tip:

*If you click **Yes** here, Access will set up an **AutoNumber** field as the primary key field. **AutoNumber** uniquely identifies a record, but tells you nothing about that record. There may be occasions when the records in a database simply need to be recorded one after the other, but usually there will be a significant and unique field or combination of fields in each record which should be used to identify that record – and that field should be chosen as the primary key.*

Checking

It is always a good idea to enter just one record in a new table to check you have set up the fields correctly.

- In the **Database** window, select the table **tblTyre** and double-click to open it.

- Type in the data shown in Figure 3.6. If all is well, well done! You have created your first table.

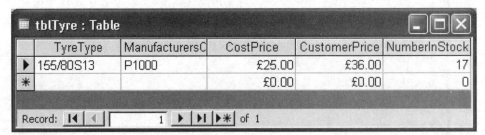

Figure 3.6

- Close **tblTyre** to return to the **Database** window.

Creating the COMPANY table

To create **tblCompany**, you can double-click **Create Table in Design View** as you did before, or you can try an alternative method:

- In the Database window, make sure the **Tables** tab is selected and click on the **New** icon. A dialogue box will open as in Figure 3.7.

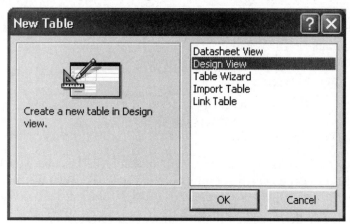

Figure 3.7

- Select **Design View**. Click **OK**.

- Enter the fields for the **Company** table. Take advantage of the **Description** column to add helpful notes.

- Set **CompanyID** as the primary key.

- Save the table with the name **tblCompany** and close it.

Your finished table should look like Figure 3.8.

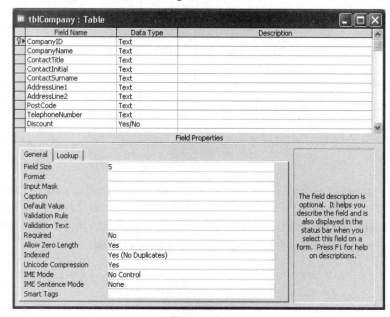

Figure 3.8

- In the **Database** window, double-click **tblCompany** to open it and enter the following data:

Attribute	Contents
CompanyID	EUR01
CompanyName	EuroHire
ContactTitle	Mr
ContactInitial	B
ContactSurname	Patten
AddressLine1	42, Industrial Way
AddressLine2	Dean
PostCode	GU12 0LD
TelephoneNumber	01267 645345
Discount	Yes

If you cannot enter the **Postcode** fully, it will probably be because you have only allowed 7 characters for the post code, which does not permit a space between the first and second group of characters.

For **Discount**, click on the checkbox for **Yes**, or leave unchecked for **No**. In your finished database, you will want some records with and some without discounts.

Linking tables

You have now created **tblTyre** and **tblCompany**. Before creating the next two tables, let's review the database design.

The entity-relationship diagram drawn in Chapter 1 is reproduced below:

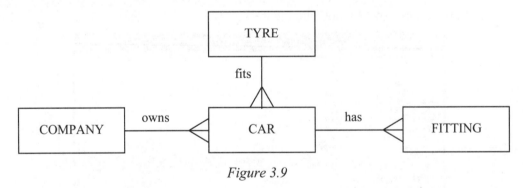

Figure 3.9

You will see that you now need to create tables for CAR (**tblCar**) and FITTING (**tblFitting**). There is no link between **tblTyre** and **tblCompany**, but we have to set up links between **tblCompany** and **tblCar**, between **tblTyre** and **tblCar** and between **tblCar** and **tblFitting**.

Each link is made using fields which are common to both tables.

For example:

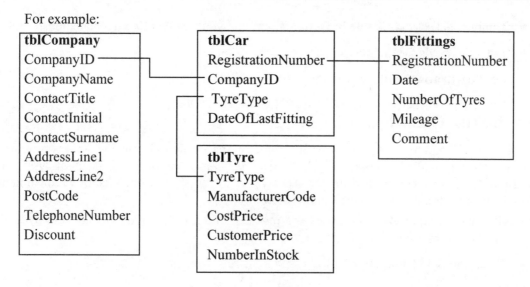

Figure 3.10

If there is a record in **tblCar** with **CompanyID EUR01**, then by looking at **tblCompany** we can see that this car belongs to *EuroHire* at *42, Industrial Way* (from the data entered at the end of Chapter 2). This is what we mean when we say the tables are 'linked by a common field'.

Foreign keys

The field **CompanyID** is the primary key of **TblCompany**. In **tblCar**, this same field is known as a *foreign key*. It is clearly an important field because it acts as a link between the two tables. It has to be defined with exactly the same data type and length in both tables, or the link will not work and Access will not be able to look up the details of the company from **tblCompany**.

Foreign key: An attribute in one table that is a primary key in another table in the database.

The CAR table

In the first chapter, the reason for dividing the details of each car between two entities **Car** and **Fitting** was discussed. You will now create these last two tables. The data types and sizes for the fields in **tblCar** are:

Field name	Data type	Field size / Format	Comments
RegistrationNumber	Text	7	Primary Key
CompanyID	Text	5	Foreign key, must exist in **tblCompany**
TyreType	Text	9	Foreign key, must exist in **tblTyre**
DateOfLastFitting	Date/Time	MediumDate	

Table 3.1

- Double-click **Create Table in Design View**, and you will be offered a blank table.

- Enter the fields for **tblCar** as in Table 3.1.

- Set **RegistrationNumber** as the primary key field.

Using a lookup wizard

The foreign key feature is dependent on the names being entered identically. Access provides a special data type called **Lookup** which is ideal for this situation, as instead of typing the **CompanyID** into a record in **tblCar**, the user will be able to select from a list of valid Company IDs which have already been entered in **tblCompany**.

We will make **CompanyID** and **TyreType** into the **Lookup** data type. Doing this will also minimise the risk of typing errors by the user.

- Select the field **CompanyID** by clicking in its row selector.

- Amend its data type to **Lookup Wizard**.

A window will appear as in Figure 3.11.

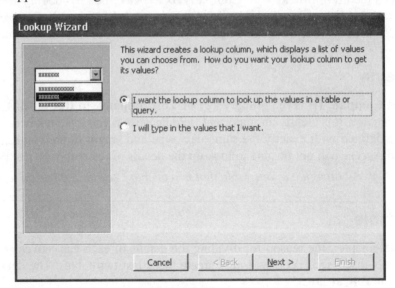

Figure 3.11

- Choose **I want the lookup column to look up the values in a table or query**. Click **Next**.

- Choose **tblCompany** as the table which will provide the values for the lookup column. Note that you have the choice of tables or queries or both here. Click **Next**.

- Choose **CompanyID**, **CompanyName** and **Address1** as the lookup fields, by selecting each in turn and clicking the > arrowhead. Click **Next**.

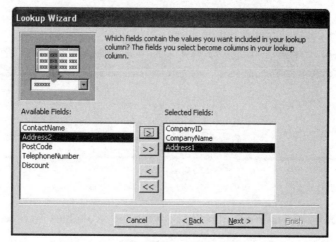

Figure 3.12

- Choose **CompanyID** and **Ascending** as the field to sort by (Access 2003 only) and click **Next**.

- Unhide the key column.

- Adjust column widths if necessary, allowing enough space for a long address line.

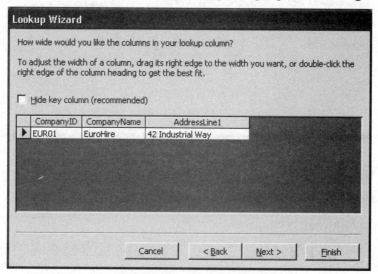

Figure 3.13

- Select **CompanyID** as the column that you want to store.

- Click **Next** again, and accept the label name **CompanyID**. Click **Finish**.

- Save the table as **tblCar**.

- To practise using the lookup facility, set up **TyreType** using a **Lookup Wizard** on **TyreType** in **tblTyre**.

- Switch to Table View by clicking the **View** icon and try using the new drop-down arrows in the **CompanyID** and **TyreType** fields.

- When you finish the **TyreType** lookup, you will get a message saying you must save in order for Access to create relationships.

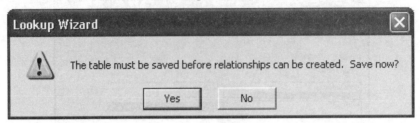

Figure 3.14

- Click **Yes**.

Access automatically creates a relationship between the two tables involved in a Lookup.

- In the menu bar click **Tools**, **Relationships**. You will see that lines connect the tables, indicating that they are linked.

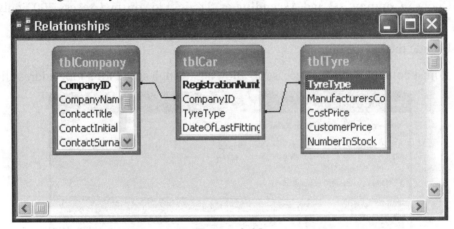

Figure 3.15

In the next chapter you will specify the type of relationships (one to many) which link the tables.

- Close the Relationships window and return to **tblCar**.

- Enter the following data:

	RegistrationNumber	CompanyID	TyreType	DateOfLastFitting
▶	GN02UGH	EUR01	155/80S13	14-Jul-04
✳				

Figure 3.16

- Save and close the table.

The FITTINGS table

The last table to be created is **tblFitting.** There is no need to specify tyre type in this table as that is unchanging, and so is stored in **tblCar.** A field for any comment that the fitter might make is included. For example, if the car was in for only two new tyres but the fitter noticed that one of the others was wearing badly, he or she would make that comment.

The outline design for this table looks like this:

Attribute	Data Type	Field length / Format	Comment
RegistrationNumber	Text	7	Joint Primary Key. LookUp from **tblCar**
FittingDate	Date / Time	Medium Date	Joint Primary Key
NumberOfTyres	Number	Byte	
Mileage	Number	Long Integer	
Comment	Memo		
InvoiceNumber	AutoNumber		

Table 3.2

Setting **RegistrationNumber** to **LookUp** from **tblCar** will reduce the risk of typographical errors and save effort.

- Start a new table in **Design View**.

- Enter **RegistrationNumber**, with a data type of **Lookup Wizard**. You need to look up the registration number from **tblCar**. Follow the steps of the wizard as before.

- Save the table as **tblFitting**. You will be asked if you want to create a primary key now. Click **No** – you will do this when you have entered the other fields.

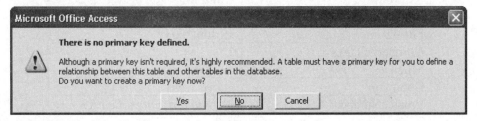

Figure 3.17

- Enter **Date**, data type **Date/Time**, format **Medium Date**. (Set the format in the **Field Properties** part of the screen, below the field names.)

- Enter **NumberOfTyres**, date type **Number**. Under **Field Properties** set the format to **Byte**.

- Enter **Mileage**, date type **Number**, **Long Integer**.

- Enter **Comment**, data type **Memo.**

- Enter **InvoiceNumber** and set its data type to **AutoNumber**.

Car registration number is insufficient as the primary key in this table, since each car could have more than one fitting, and so **RegistrationNumber** would not identify any record uniquely. A *composite* or *combined key* is required, combining registration number and fitting date.

Composite Key: A primary key that is made up of more than one attribute.

To set the composite key for this table:

- Click the row selector for **RegistrationNumber**, and hold down the **Ctrl** key while you select the **Date** row.

- Click on the **Primary Key** icon.

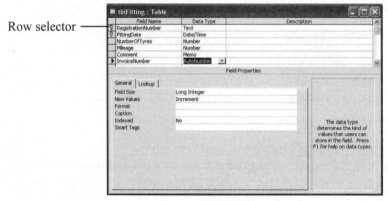

Figure 3.18

- Save the table as **tblFitting** and close it.

The tables have now been created. You have included those fields specified in the brief, and a few others that appear to be needed in order to complete the tasks described.

Enter the record below into **tblFitting** to check that there are no obvious errors in your table design.

Attribute	Contents
RegistrationNumber	GN02UGH
FittingDate	12 Jun 2003
NumberOfTyres	2
Mileage	*11,700*
Comment	*Leave blank*
InvoiceNumber	01 *(entered automatically)*

Table 3.3: tblFitting sample record

If you have made any errors in creating a table structure, open the table again in **Design View** and make corrections. You can add or delete fields and change field properties – look in the Access **Help** for guidance.

In the next chapter you will add some validation rules to fields in your tables, and set up relationships between the tables.

Chapter 4 – Constraints

Objectives

By the end of this chapter you will have:

entered validation rules and input masks on some fields;

set up one-to-many relationships between tables;

enforced referential integrity.

Validation

Validation rules can be used to reduce the chance of error during data entry. The rules are applied to data on entry, and are used to check that it is valid. For example, in a date, Access will automatically check that you have not entered 13 as a month number or 32 as a day.

It is easy to set validation rules when creating a table in Access using the **Field Properties** section in **Design View**.

Typical validation rules

Here are some typical validation rules:

	Rule	**Effect**
1	<10	Value less than 10
2	>0	Value greater than zero (positive)
3	>0 And <6	Greater than zero and less than 6
4	Between 1 And 5	Between 1 and 5 inclusive
5	<0 Or >10	Either negative or greater than 10
6	>0 Or Is Null	Either blank or positive
7	Like P????	Text is 5 characters beginning with P
8	Like P*	Text is 1 or more characters beginning with P

Note:

If you set an input mask (validation rule) on a field, Access does not allow that field to be blank unless you add **Or Is Null** in your input mask as in Rule 6 above.

There are two characters used as *wild cards* in Access.

?   a single character   as in Rule 7 above

*   any number of characters   as in Rule 8.

Entering a validation rule

In the Tod's Tyres exercise, the number of tyres fitted must not exceed five. Clearly the number of tyres fitted cannot be negative or zero, so you want to restrict the data entered in this field to between 1 and 5.

- From the Database window, open **tblFitting** in Design View.

- Select **NumberOfTyres:** move the cursor to **Validation Rule** in the **Field Properties** section.

- Type *Between 1 And 5 Or Is Null*

- Enter an explanatory message in the line below that will explain to a user why his entry of *6* has not been accepted.

- To test your rule, switch to **Datasheet View**. You will be asked if you wish to save the changes to the table design. Select **Yes**.

- You will probably see this message:

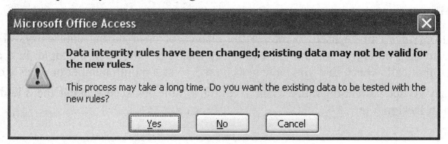

Figure 4.1

- Select **Yes**.

- Enter a record for a fitting. Enter *6* as the number of tyres. When you try to tab out of the record you will see an error message:

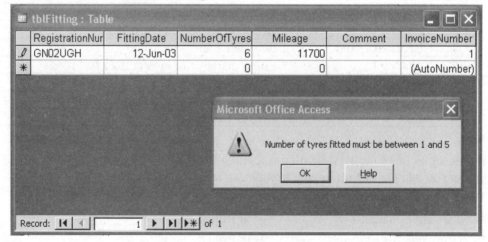

Figure 4.2

- Enter *2* so that your validation rule will be obeyed and the record saved.

Input masks

The letters in a car registration number are in upper case. You could use the **Shift** or **Caps Lock** key every time when entering this data, but Access can make things easier for you with an input mask. This will also help reduce the chances of an error.

Some of the characters that are used in an input mask are given below. The really useful characters have been emboldened at the top of the table.

Character	Description
0	**Digit (0 to 9, entry required, plus [+] and minus [–] signs not allowed).**
9	**Digit or space (entry not required, plus and minus signs not allowed).**
L	**Letter (A to Z, entry required).**
?	**Letter (A to Z, entry optional).**
<	**Causes all characters to be converted to lowercase.**
>	**Causes all characters to be converted to uppercase.**
\	Causes the character that follows to be displayed as the literal character (for example, \A is displayed as just A).
A	Letter or digit (entry required).
a	Letter or digit (entry optional).
&	Any character or a space (entry required).
C	Any character or a space (entry optional).
#	Digit or space (entry not required; spaces are displayed as blanks while in Edit mode, but blanks are removed when data is saved; plus and minus signs allowed).

Table 4.2

The format of the car registration number is CCNNCCC, where C denotes an upper case letter and N a digit. So the input mask for the registration number would be:

>	LL	00	LLL
To convert all characters to upper case	For 2 required characters	For 2 required digits	For 3 required characters

Entering the input mask

- Open **tblCar** in **Design View**.

- Select the **RegistrationNumber**.

- Select **Input Mask** in the **Field Properties**, and type *>LL00LLL* as the input mask.

- Close the table, saving the changes.

Testing the validation rule

- In the **Database** window, double-click **tblCar** to open it.

- Try to enter an invalid car registration number such as *NX3DEV*. The input mask should prevent it.

- Re-enter it as *nx03dev*. The input mask should change the letters to uppercase.

- Choose **EuroHire** from the drop-down **Company** list.

- Choose a **TyreType** of **155/80S13**. Leave **DateOfLastFitting** blank.

- Close the table.

Relationships

The four entities for which you have created tables are connected by the following relationships:

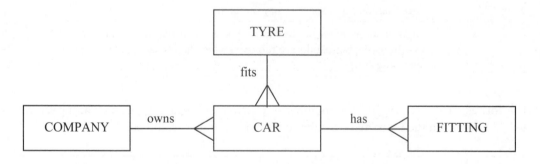

Figure 4.3

You need to ensure that these four relationships have been created in your database.

- From the menu bar select **Tools, Relationships** or click the **Relationships** icon.

Figure 4.3 shows you what relationships should be set. The **Relationships** window may be blank or some but not all tables may be showing. Because we have used **Lookup** fields, Access knows that the tables are linked in some way.

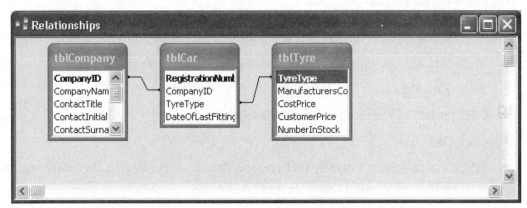

Figure 4.4

You need to add **tblFitting**, as follows:

- Click the **Show Table** icon.

- Select **tblFitting** and click **Add**.

- Close the **Show Table** window.

To create a one-to-many relationship between **tblCar** and **tblFitting**:

- Drag **RegistrationNumber** from **tblCar** to **tblFitting**. (Always drag from the **one** to the **many** side of the relationship. One Car has many Fittings.)

- Access will offer you a dialogue box with a suggested relationship:

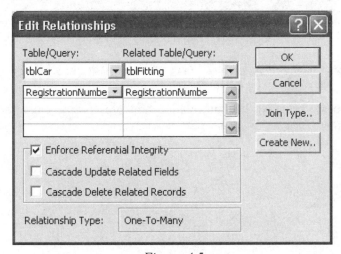

Figure 4.5

- Click the box **Enforce Referential Integrity**. This will ensure that it is impossible to enter a fitting for a non-existing car.

- Leave the other boxes for now. Click **OK**.

Enforcing referential integrity

Referential integrity ensures that you cannot, for example, add a car for a non-existent company or book a fitting for a non-existent car.

Enforce Referential Integrity has not yet been set between **tblCompany** and **tblCar** – in Figure 4.4, the link between the tables is not specific. You can edit the relationship:

- Right-click the line showing the relationship between the relevant tables.

- Select **Edit Relation**.

- Click the box to **Enforce Referential Integrity**.

- Click **OK**.

- Edit the relationship between **tblTyre** and **tblCar**, according to the entity relationship diagram in Figure 4.3.

Your finished relationship window should look like this.

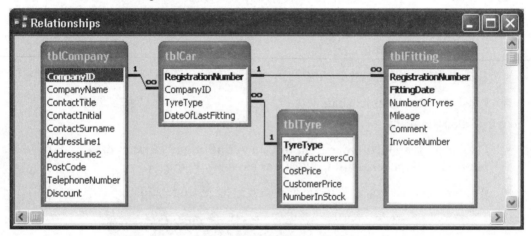

Figure 4.6

Tip:

This is NOT an entity relationship diagram. If you are asked to draw an ER diagram in an examination, you should draw Figure 4.3, not Figure 4.6.

- When you are satisfied that the relationships are correct, close the window, saving the relationships.

Chapter 5 – Forms for Data Entry

Objectives

By the end of this chapter you will have:

created data entry forms for the user to enter data;

entered test data to try out the forms.

User interfaces

A good user interface for data entry is designed to be easy on the eye, and to enable the user to enter data correctly and efficiently.

Data can be entered directly into tables, as you have already seen. However, for a large number of fields this would involve scrolling across the screen, which is not efficient or user-friendly. Instead, a form can be designed for data entry, which can accept data and then automatically store it in the correct table.

What forms?

From the list of objectives you can see that Tod will use form user interfaces for the following tasks:

Task	Data required
Enter details of a new company	Company name, address & telephone number, contact name
Enter details of a new car	Registration number, tyre type, company name
Book a tyre fitting	Registration number, date, number of tyres required
Check that the right tyre is in stock	Tyre type, number in stock, number required
Enter a comment, if necessary, as a result of a fitting and update the **DateOfLastFitting** field.	Registration number, date, mileage, comment
Update tyre price list	Tyre type, manufacturer's code, customer price

Table 5.1

There are many different ways of organizing your forms, and deciding what data to have in what forms. The suggestions that follow are not a 'best' option. They have been chosen to keep the exercise fairly simple, assuming that you may be learning Access as you go along.

This solution will use four forms for the tasks described in Table 5.1, together with a type of menu form called a *switchboard* which will be created in Chapter 8. The forms will be as follows:

Form	Task	Data	From Tables
frmCompany	To register a new company	Company ID & name, address & telephone number, contact name	tblCompany
frmCar	To register a new car	Registration number, Company ID & name, contact name, tyre type, number in stock	tblCar, tblTyre
frmFitting	Book a Fitting Check tyres in stock Record a comment in a fitting	Registration number, date, company name, contact name, tyre type, number of tyres required, number in stock, mileage, comment, date of last fitting	tblCar, tblFitting, tblTyre, tblCompany
frmTyre	Update price list	All fields in tblTyre	tblTyre
Switchboard	Menu		

Table 5.2

Using the form wizard

The first task that you will need to be able to do is to enter details of a new customer. This needs a simple form, with all the required data taken from only one table. The Form Wizard will help you create a form based on a table or query.

- From the **Database** window, select the **Forms** tab.

- Select **Create form by using a wizard.**

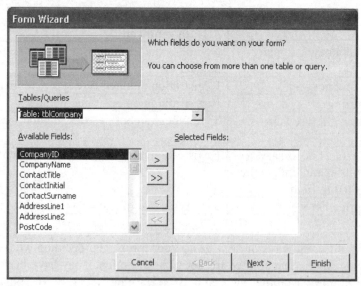

Figure 5.1

- Select **tblCompany**. All available fields will be offered.

- Click the double-headed arrow to select them all. (This form will be used for entering details of a new customer, so all details are needed.) Click **Next**.

- Click **Next** again to select a columnar layout.

- Choose your background – the colour can be altered later.

- Enter **frmCompany** (not **tblCompany**) as a title. This will be the name of the form which you will see in the **Database** window.

- Accept the default of opening the form to enter data. (You want to see what it looks like before modifying the design.)

- Click **Finish**.

If you entered data to check your Company table when you created that, your first record should be showing.

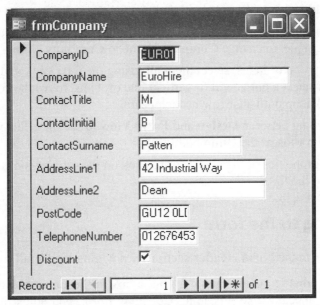

Figure 5.2

Improvements can be made to this form. For example:

♦ The spaces allowed for **TelephoneNumber** and **PostCode** are too short;

♦ The form should have a title stating its purpose;

♦ A button could be added to enable the user to close the form.

Modifying a form

Access offers many tools for modifying a form, and the best way to learn which of these will be most useful is simply to experiment.

To give you a start, here are a few pointers:

♦ You can extend the form in **Design View** both horizontally and vertically by holding the cursor over the edge until it appears as ↔or ↕.

♦ If you click on a field and hold down the left mouse button, you see an **open hand**. You can move both the field and its label *together*.

♦ If you click on the top left corner of either a field or its label you see a **hand with a pointing finger**. You can move that object *separately*.

♦ If you select the **Properties** icon, you can access the object properties. Here you can see and amend all the properties of the selected object, such as colour, font, alignment, border, height, width, what to do 'on click' and many more.

♦ You can use the **Object Properties** to change the labels from the field names to ordinary text; for example, to change **CompanyName** to **Company Name**.

♦ To *align* a group of items, select them all (using the **Ctrl** key), and press the right mouse button. To select a horizontal or vertical line of items, move the cursor to the left hand side or to the top until an arrow head appears.

♦ Keep switching between **Design** and **Form View** to see the effect your amendments are having. Don't forget the **Undo** button!

♦ To see the properties of the whole form, click on the square alongside the horizontal ruler at the top of the form.

Adding a heading to the form

● Make space in the **Form Header** section by dragging the **Detail** line down.

● Click the **Label** icon, and then drag out a box in the **Form Header** where you want the heading to appear. Type a heading *Company Form*, and adjust its size, justification and font.

Adding a button

● Make space in the **Form Footer** section by dragging the **Form Footer** line down.

● If the **Toolbox** is not open, click on the **Toolbox** icon in the toolbar.

● Select the **Button** icon.

● Using the cursor, draw out a button in a suitable position.

● Select **Form Operations**, then select **Close Form**. Click **Next**.

● Accept the closing door picture, or type in your own text. Click **Next**.

● Name the button *btnCloseForm* so that it will remind you what it does, and click **Finish**.

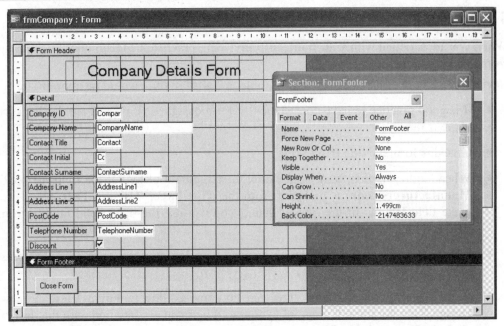

Figure 5.3

- Now switch to **Form View** and enter the names of the companies given in the test data shown below.

Company ID	Company Name	Contact	Contact	Contact	Address Line 1	Address Line 2	PostCode	Telephone Num	Discount
EUR01	EuroHire	Mr	B	Patten	42 Industrial Way	Dean	GU12 0LD	01267645345	☑
EXP01	Express Hire	Mrs	B	Jones	Station Approach	Cambertown	GU13 5GH	01267377377	☐
MAK01	Make Way Motors	Mr	J	Pierce	37 Thatcham Road	Catford	RG21 3RB	01183672345	☐
▶ MAS01	Masterson Taxis	Ms	B	Masters	112 New Road	Sunningfield	RG12 4GH	01181236576	☑
PAY01	Payne Cars	Mr	O	Heath	12 Old Street	Bramley	GU24 3SW	01234567812	☑
WES01	West Heath Services	Mr	M	Gower	221 Gordon Road	West Heath	GU21 7BH	01932354857	☐
*									▨

Figure 5.4

Your form should look something like this:

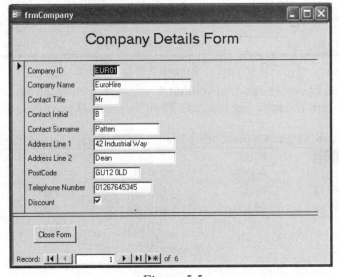

Figure 5.5

The Tyre form

When you are satisfied with your **frmCompany** form, practise the techniques by creating a form from the **Tyre** table.

In view of the type of data needed for this table, a **Tabular** style would be appropriate.

- It is good practice to have consistency of form design, so choose a similar background for all your forms.

- Give this form the title **frmTyres.**

- When modifying this form, notice how the alignment of two of the fields (**TyreType** and **ManufacturersCode**) is different from the other three. Use the **Text Align** property to make field lengths fit the typical data. You can use the open hand facility to move the field and its label together.

- Use the handles on the label boxes and the **Caption** property to improve the presentation of the field headings.

- With Access 2000 and 2003, you can do some editing in **Form View**. You will need **Design View** for the full range of features. When you are satisfied with the design, simply close the **Properties** box using the **X**.

- Add a **Close Form** button in the **Footer** section of the form. For consistency, it should be the same size and in the same position as the one in the Company form. Note that in a form in tabular format you *must* put the button in the **Footer**.

- Your finished form could look like this:

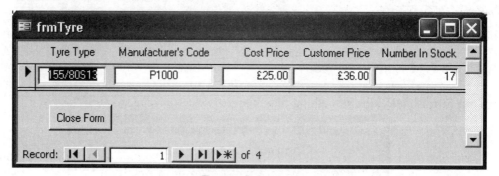

Figure 5.6

To check that you can enter data into your table via a form, enter the data for the other three tyre types using the form you have just created. Then look at **tblTyre** to see that the data is there.

TyreType	ManufacturersCode	CostPrice	CustomerPrice	NumberInStock
155/80S13	P1000	£25.00	£36.00	17
165/80S13	P3000	£30.00	£39.00	14
155/80S14	P5000	£44.50	£58.50	21
165/80S14	P7000	£49.00	£64.00	11
*		£0.00	£0.00	0

Figure 5.7

To enter a new record on a form in Tabular format, just press the **Tab** key at the end of the previous record. Alternatively, select the **New record** button at the bottom of the form.

There is little to choose between a table and a form for this small amount of data entry. A form is most useful when there is a lot of data for each record, or for combining data entry into more than one table, as you will see from the next step.

Hints for form design

Now that you have some idea of what can be done with forms, you should think about the overall design of forms for your exercise. Here are some criteria for good form design which you should consider.

♦ Choose a combination of background and text colours which are clear and easy to read, in all expected light levels.

♦ Don't put too much information onto one screen; if you have to have too many fields on a form, consider spreading these over two forms.

♦ Don't make your screen too 'busy'; choose no more than two or three different fonts and colours.

♦ If you have more than one form in a project, you should aim for consistency of background colour, text colour and font.

♦ If you have more than one form in a project, you should aim for consistency of layout, for example by always putting a **Close** button in the same place.

Forms from more than one table

The **Car** form requires fields from two different tables.

● From the **Forms** tab, select **Create Form by using wizard**. You will be offered **tblCar** (as that is the first alphabetically).

● Select all the fields for inclusion, using the double-headed arrow.

● Select **tblCompany**.

● Select **ContactTitle, ContactInitial, ContactSurname** and **CompanyName** from this table individually, using the single-headed arrow. Click **Next**.

● Access suggests you want to view your data by car: accept this suggestion. It is so easy to create a form using the wizard that, if the finished result is not what you want, you can delete it and start again!

● Click **Next**.

● Click **Next** to accept **Columnar**.

● Select your (consistent) background and click **Next**.

● Enter **frmCar** as a title and click **Finish**.

When you look at this form, you will probably decide it can be improved. The information is too crowded together and not arranged logically.

It is easier to assess the layout of a form if you have some data, so if you have not already done so, switch to **Form View** ready to enter some data.

The test data is shown below:

Registration	Company ID	Tyre Type	Date Of Last Fitting	Company Name	Contact Title	Contact Initial	Contact Surname
BR02SWL	PAY01	165/80S14		Payne Cars	Mr	O	Heath
BR03DEV	PAY01	155/80S14		Payne Cars	Mr	O	Heath
GN02UGH	EUR01	155/80S13		EuroHire	Mr	B	Patten
GN03YES	EUR01	165/80S13		EuroHire	Mr	B	Patten
GR04FLK	EUR01	165/80S14		EuroHire	Mr	B	Patten
GU03WIN	WES01	155/80S13		West Heath Services	Mr	M	Gower
GX03DEX	EUR01	155/80S13		EuroHire	Mr	B	Patten
NX03DEV	EUR01	155/80S13		EuroHire	Mr	B	Patten
RG03FRD	MAS01	155/80S13		Masterson Taxis	Ms	B	Masters
RG03NOW	MAK01	155/80S13		Make Way Motors	Mr	J	Pierce
RG51DDL	MAS01	155/80S14		Masterson Taxis	Ms	B	Masters
RG52SWE	MAS01	155/80S13		Masterson Taxis	Ms	B	Masters
RG53ABC	MAK01	165/80S13		Make Way Motors	Mr	J	Pierce
RG53NPW	MAK01	165/80S14		Make Way Motors	Mr	J	Pierce
SL52OUG	EXP01	155/80S14		Express Hire	Mrs	B	Jones
SL53OGH	EXP01	165/80S14		Express Hire	Mrs	B	Jones

Figure 5.8

- By switching between **Design** and **Form View**, modify the layout of this form.

Suggestions for improvement

You can extend the form in width or height to spread things out. Figure 5.9 shows one suggested layout.

♦ Fields have been moved, so that the **Company Name** and **Contact Name** are together.

♦ Tyre information is together.

♦ Some field lengths have been altered.

♦ Attention has been paid to the alignment of fields and to the presentation of the labels.

♦ A title has been added to the **Form Header**. Similar titles will be added to all forms.

♦ A button to close the form has been added in the **Footer**.

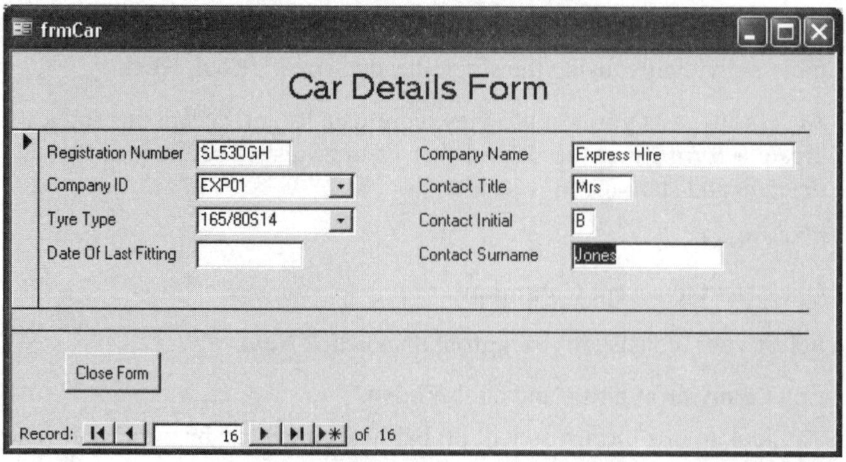

Figure 5.9

The Fittings form

This last form will take data from all four tables. When a fitting is done, the field **DateOfLastFitting** will be entered as the current date and automatically stored in the Car table.

- Select **Create form by using wizard**.

- Select **tblFitting** and all fields from this table

- Select additional fields from the other tables as follows (you can select these fields either by double-clicking them or by using the single–headed arrow):
    - from **tblCar**: **CompanyID**, **TyreType**, **DateOfLastFitting**;
    - from **tblTyre**: **NumberInStock**;
    - from **tblCompany**: **CompanyName**, **ContactName**.

- Click **Next**.

- Try all the options of viewing the data to see what difference they make, then select **by tblFitting**.

- Click **Next**.

- Choose a **Columnar** layout and click **Next**.

- Select your usual background and click **Next**.

- Name the form **frmfitting** and click **Finish**.

- When the wizard has produced a form, modify it.
    - Place related fields together, as in Figure 5.15.
    - Add a button to close the form.
    - Add a title to be consistent with the other forms you have created.

- Use the form to add the following data:

	Registration Number	Fitting Date	Number Of Tyres	Mileage	Comment	Invoice	Company ID	Tyre Type	Date Of Last Fitting
▶	GN02UGH	12-Jun-03	2	11700		1	EUR01	155/80S13	14-Jul-04
	BR02SWL	12-May-03	2	24657		2	PAY01	165/80S14	11-Jun-04
	RG51DDL	01-Jul-03	2	34887		3	MAS01	155/80S14	01-Jul-03
	SL53OGH	02-Jul-03	3	12687		4	EXP01	165/80S14	02-Jul-03
	GN02UGH	11-Jul-03	4	15210		5	EUR01	155/80S13	14-Jul-04
	RG52SWE	01-Aug-03	1	24866		6	MAS01	155/80S13	01-Aug-03
	BR03DEV	02-Aug-03	3	8420		7	PAY01	155/80S14	02-Aug-03
	GX03DEX	07-May-04	3	16883		8	EUR01	155/80S13	07-May-04
	RG03NOW	11-Jun-04	4	18520		9	MAK01	155/80S13	11-Jun-04
	BR02SWL	11-Jun-04	3	28630		10	PAY01	165/80S14	11-Jun-04
	GN02UGH	14-Jul-04	3	31650	Tracking out of alignment	11	EUR01	155/80S13	14-Jul-04
	GU03WIN	16-Jul-04	4	15990	Uneven wear on near side	12	WES01	155/80S13	16-Jul-04
*					lumber)				

Figure 5.10

Remember that when a car comes in for a fitting, the **DateOfLastFitting** field will be changed to be the same as the **FittingDate**. You will see this happening, for example, in the case of car GN02UGH which has had a second and third fitting. When you enter the data in the first record, you can enter **DateOfLastFitting** as 12-Jun-03. The data in this record will be changed automatically when you enter the next record for the same car with a different **DateOfLastFitting**.

Processing steps

You need to think through what happens when a customer rings up to book a fitting, and when the fitting is actually done. The steps in this solution will be as follows:

1. When a booking is made, Tod opens the Fittings form and goes to a new record.

2. He enters the data and checks that there are sufficient tyres in stock. In a more sophisticated solution, there would be two fields instead of one for **number in stock**; one field for **free stock** and one field for **allocated stock**, which would both be adjusted when the booking was made. In this simple solution, the number in stock is updated manually, probably when the booking is made.

3. When the car comes in for its fitting, Tod needs to look on the Fittings form to find the record that was created at the time of booking. The easiest way to do this is to put the cursor in the field for **RegistrationNumber**, find the first record for the car and then click **Find the Next Record** until the latest Fitting record is found.

4. Two copies of the invoice are printed.

A button to find a record

We will add a button to the Fittings form to find a record for a particular car. First of all try the operation manually. You need to place the cursor in the **RegistrationNumber** field, and then click the **Find** button on the toolbar. You now need to type in the registration number you are looking for.

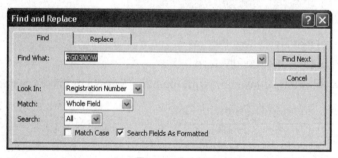

Figure 5.11

In order to get Access to do this automatically, you need to place a button on the form which puts the cursor in the correct field and then displays the **Find** window. First of all, we will place the **Find** button.

- With **frmFitting** in **Design View**, select the **Button** icon from the toolbox and place a button in the **Form Footer** next to the **Close Form** button.

- With category **Record Navigation**, choose **Find Record**.

- Enter *Find Car* as the text to appear on the button.

- Name the button *btnFindCar*. Click **Finish**.

- Go to **Form View** and put your cursor in the first field on the form. Then test your button. The problem is, if the cursor is not in the field for **RegistrationNumber**, it will not work properly.

One way to solve this problem is to take the plunge and add a line of VBA code to the procedure which the wizard has automatically generated for the button.

Creating an event procedure

- In **Design View**, right-click the **FindCar** button and open the **Properties** window.

- Go to the **On Click** event, and click the three dots that appear on the right-hand side.

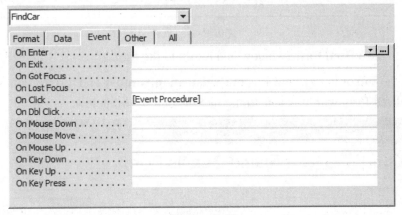

Figure 5.12

- Select **Code Builder** and press **OK**.

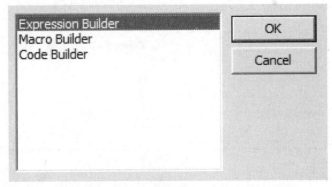

Figure 5.13

The **Code** window will appear. This shows all the code that has been automatically generated for you by the **Button Wizard**. You can insert one line of code to set the focus in the right field before the **Find** window is opened. Note that:

- The new line that you will enter will replace the line

    Screen.PreviousControl.SetFocus

- Instead of deleting this line, it is safer to simply turn it into a comment, which will be ignored by the compiler when running the code. To do this, type a quote mark (') in front of the line.

    The comment will appear in green.

- Above it, enter the new line to set the focus to the **RegistrationNumber** field:
  RegistrationNumber.SetFocus

New code

```
Private Sub FindCar_Click()
On Error GoTo Err_FindCar_Click

    RegistrationNumber.SetFocus
    'Screen.PreviousControl.SetFocus
    DoCmd.DoMenuItem acFormBar, acEditMenu, 10, , acMenuVer70
```

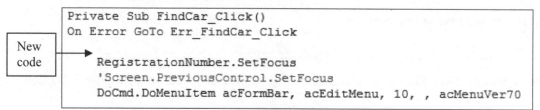

Figure 5.14

- Close the **Visual Basic** window and return to the form.
- Put the cursor in any field except **RegistrationNumber** and test the button.

The completed form will look something like the one shown below:

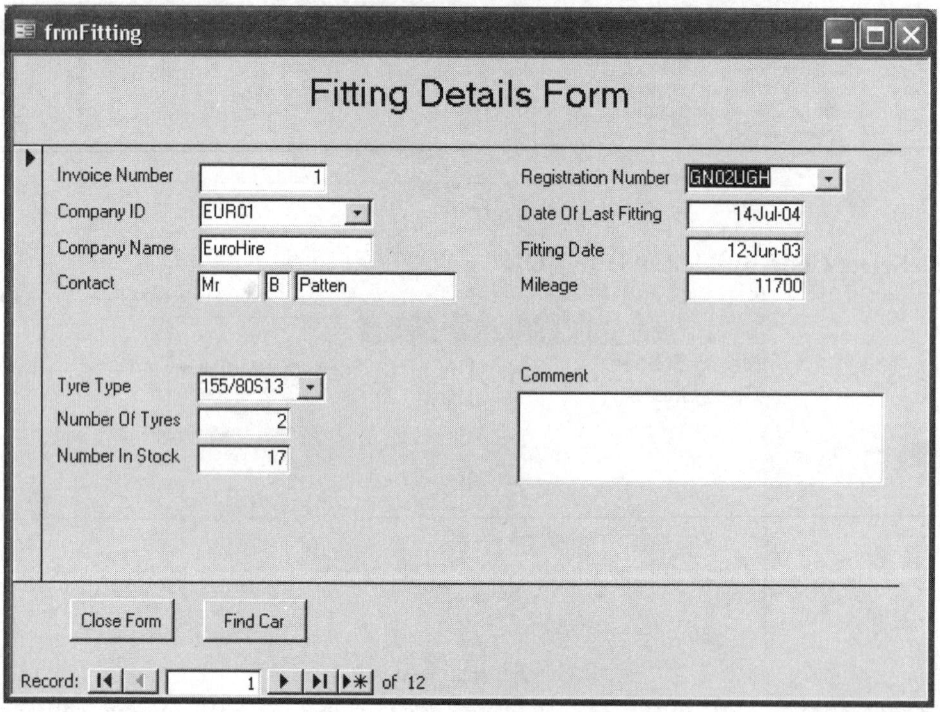

Figure 5.15

Test all your forms thoroughly to make sure that they work correctly. You may find that, because you have moved fields around on a form, the cursor does not move to the next field when you press the **Tab** key. To correct this you need to change the **Tab Order**.

Changing the Tab order

- With **frmFitting** in **Design View**, select **View, Tab Order**.

- Select the **Detail** section.

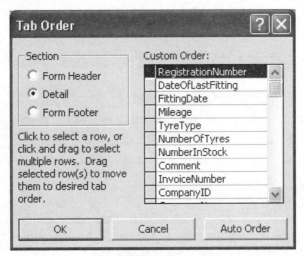

Figure 5.16

To select an item, click in the box to the left of that item. You need to put the items in the list in the same sequence as you would expect a user to fill them in on the form. The quickest way of doing this is to use the **Auto Order** button.

- Click the **Auto Order** button, and then click **OK**.

Test the form again. If the tab order is still not correct, you can alter it manually by clicking to the left of the field name in the **Tab Order** window to select it, and then dragging it to the correct position.

Chapter 6 – Queries

Objectives

By the end of this chapter you will have:

created queries using criteria, parameters, calculations and summary functions;

created queries for the reminder letter and the invoice.

The reminder letter

Once a month, Tod wants his new system to select those cars which have not had tyres fitted for a year, so that he can send reminder letters. This could be done either by using a mail merge in Word, or by creating a report including the text of a letter.

We will not actually produce the standard letter in this sample task, but we will prepare for it.

You need to start by selecting the specific cars. This will be done using a query, which will search the Fittings table for those cars which had new tyres fitted a year ago. As this is done once a month, we will look for records which were last fitted with tyres between 350 and 380 days ago.

Creating the query

Queries are used in Access to extract certain data by searching one or more tables for records which meet certain criteria.

Here are the fields we need to include in the query:

Field	From Table
DateOfLastFitting	tblCar
RegistrationNumber	tblCar
CompanyName	tblCompany
TyreType	tblCar
ContactTitle	tblCompany
ContactInitial	tblCompany
ContactSurname	tblCompany
Address1	tblCompany
Address2	tblCompany
PostCode	tblCompany
Discount	tblCompany
CustomerPrice	tblTyre

Table 6.1

- From the **Database** window, double-click **Create Query in Design View**. You will see the following window:

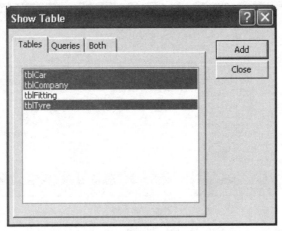

Figure 6.1

- Select **tblCar** and hold down the **Ctrl** key while you select **tblCompany** and **tblTyre**. Then click **Add**, followed by **Close**.

The **Query** window appears, showing the tables you selected. You can arrange the tables and adjust the size of the top half of the window as well as resize the whole window.

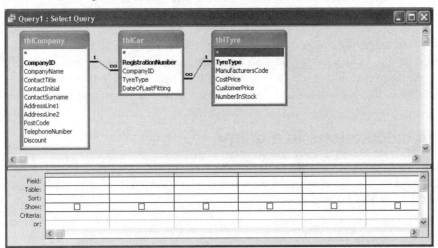

Figure 6.2

Now you need to drag the fields that you need onto the query grid in the bottom half of the window.

- Drag all the fields from the correct tables (as shown in Table 6.1) onto the query grid.

Your query grid should look like this (not all the fields are shown in the figure below):

DateOfLastFitting	RegistrationNumber	CompanyName	TyreType	ContactTitle	ContactInitial	ContactSurname	AddressLine1	AddressLine2	PostCode	Disc
tblCar	tblCar	tblCompany	tblTyre	tblCompany	tblCompany	tblCompany	tblCompany	tblCompany	tblCompan	tblC
☑	☑	☑	☑	☑	☑	☑	☑	☑	☑	

Figure 6.3

- Now click the **Run** button to test the query.

You will see all the records displayed in a table:

Figure 6.4

You can use this table as the basis of a report or form.

- Save the query, giving it the name *qryReminder*. Don't close the query yet because it needs more work!

- In **Design View**, click in the Criteria row of the **DateOfLastFitting** column.

- Enter the criterion *Between Date()-350 and Date()-380*.

Note that **Date()** gives today's date.

- Run the query again, and check that the records which appear are about a month either side of one year ago. If you don't get any records showing, you probably need to enter some more test data with dates that match this criterion. You also need to make sure that you have data for at least one customer who gets a discount and one who does not.

Performing calculations in a query

You can use queries to do calculations for you. In the reminder letter, Tod could give the customer a quote for the cost of fitting each tyre for a particular car, applying a discount if the **Discount** field is **Yes** for that customer.

To get the discounted cost for these customers, you need an **Iif** function. The discount will be 5% of the **CustomerPrice** if the discount applies, and zero otherwise.

- In **Design View**, enter a new field in the query grid named **DiscountValue** as follows:

PostCode	Discount	CustomerPrice	DiscountValue: IIf([Discount],[CustomerPrice]*0.05,0)	
tblCompan	tblCompany	tblTyre		
☑	☑	☑	☑	☐

Figure 6.5

Note: The formula

Iif(Discount, CustomerPrice*0.05,0)

is interpreted as:

If Discount=True

Then DiscountValue =CustomerPrice*0.05

Else DiscountValue = 0

The new field name **DiscountValue** is specified by putting it at the beginning of the formula, followed by a colon as shown.

- Run the query again to test it.

Check that the discount has been correctly calculated for all customers.

We can also calculate the net cost after applying the discount, and VAT on the discounted cost.

The formula for the Net cost is: *NetCost:(CustomerPrice - DiscountValue)*

The formula for VAT is: *VAT:(0.175 * NetCost)*

The formula for Total cost is: *TotalCost:(NetCost + VAT)*

You can insert these fields yourself.

Fomatting fields in a query

The new fields need to be formatted as **Currency**. Access will recognise that some are currency, but perhaps not all of them.

- To reformat any that are not shown as currency fields, right-click the field name in the query grid and select **Properties**.

- Set the **Format** property to **Currency**, and **Decimal Places** to *2*.

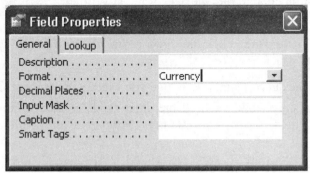

Figure 6.6

- Save your query and return to the **Database** window.

The steps for doing the mail merge are not shown here.

Using summary functions in a query

We will look at a second example of a query, which will show some of the other useful things that queries can do. This query will provide an alternative method of finding out when a car last had a fitting, without using the **DateOfLastFitting** field.

- Double-click **Create Query in Design View** and add **tblFitting** to the query window.

- Add all the fields to the query grid and run the query to test it.

RegistrationNumber	FittingDate	NumberOfTyres	Mileage	Comment	InvoiceNumber
BR02SWL	12-May-03	2	24657		2
BR02SWL	11-Jun-04	3	28630		10
BR03DEV	02-Aug-03	3	8420		7
GN02UGH	12-Jun-03	2	11700		1
GN02UGH	11-Jul-03	4	15210		5
GN02UGH	14-Jul-04	3	31650	Tracking out of alignment	11
GU03WIN	26-Jul-03	4	15990	Uneven wear on near side	12
GX03DEX	07-May-04	3	16883		8
RG03NOW	11-Jun-04	4	18520		9
RG51DDL	01-Jul-03	2	34887		3
RG52SWE	01-Aug-03	1	24866		6
SL53OGH	02-Jul-03	3	12687		4
*		0	0		(AutoNumber)

Record: I◄ ◄ [1] ► ►I ►* of 12

Figure 6.7

You will see that some cars have had more than one fitting. We would not want to send a reminder to the owner of car BR02SW1, for example, because although they had a fitting over a year ago, they have had another one since.

We can use the **last** function to find the date of the last fitting.

- Return to **Design View** and click the **Totals** button to bring up the **Total** row. In the column for **FittingDate**, click the down-arrow next to **Group By**, scroll down select the function **last**.

- Try running the query again. It will give you exactly the same result.

Summary functions only work when all the other fields contain identical data. Therefore, you need to remove the fields for **NumberOfTyres**, **Mileage**, **Comment** and **InvoiceNumber** from the query grid.

- Right-click in the row header of each field and select **Cut**.

- Now run the query again. You will see the following results:

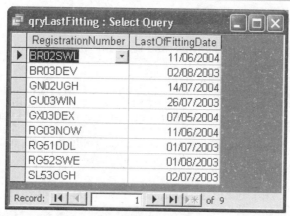

Figure 6.8

Note that Access automatically gives a field name **LastOfFittingDate** to the new field.

- Save the query as *qryLastFitting* and return to the **Database** window.

You can try out some of the other summary functions yourself. Then clear the function in the **Total** row and try sorting fields in a different sequence using the **Sort** button to bring up a new row. You can sort on more than one row, but Access sorts fields by default from left to right, so you may need to move the fields around if you want a different sort order.

You can also specify which fields you want to show in the **Query Results** table.

The Invoice query

The invoice will be created as a report.

The data required in the invoice is specified in the brief. All four tables are required.

Field	From Table
InvoiceNumber	tblFitting
FittingDate	tblFitting
CompanyName	tblCompany
AddressLine1	tblCompany
AddressLine2	tblCompany
PostCode	tblCompany
Telephone Number	tblCompany
ContactTitle	tblCompany
ContactInitial	tblCompany
ContactSurname	tblCompany
RegistrationNumber	tblFitting
NumberOfTyres	tblFitting
TyreType	tblCar
CustomerPrice	tblTyre
Discount	tblCompany
VAT	Calculated field

Table 6.2

A Parameter Query

An invoice refers to one particular fitting, and so to one particular fitting record. A parameter query is ideal for this situation.

- From the **Database** window double-click **Create Query in Design View**.

- Add the four tables **tblCar, tblCompany, tblFitting** and **tblTyres**

- Select the fields from the tables as specified in Table 6.2 and add them to the query grid.

- Save the query as **qryInvoice**.

- Run the query. You should get a number of records as shown in Figure 6.9.

InvoiceNumber	FittingDate	CompanyName	AddressLine1	AddressLine2	PostCode	TelephoneNumber	ContactTitle	ContactInitial	ContactSurname
1	12-Jun-03	EuroHire	42 Industrial Way	Dean	GU12 0LD	01267645345	Mr	B	Patten
5	11-Jul-03	EuroHire	42 Industrial Way	Dean	GU12 0LD	01267645345	Mr	B	Patten
11	14-Jul-04	EuroHire	42 Industrial Way	Dean	GU12 0LD	01267645345	Mr	B	Patten
2	12-May-03	Payne Cars	12 Old Street	Bramley	GU24 3SW	01234567812	Mr	O	Heath
10	11-Jun-04	Payne Cars	12 Old Street	Bramley	GU24 3SW	01234567812	Mr	O	Heath
7	02-Aug-03	Payne Cars	12 Old Street	Bramley	GU24 3SW	01234567812	Mr	O	Heath
12	26-Jul-03	West Heath Services	221 Gordon Road	West Heath	GU21 7BH	01932354857	Mr	M	Gower
8	07-May-04	EuroHire	42 Industrial Way	Dean	GU12 0LD	01267645345	Mr	B	Patten
9	11-Jun-04	Make Way Motors	37 Thatcham Road	Catford	RG21 3RB	01183672345	Mr	J	Pierce
3	01-Jul-03	Masterson Taxis	112 New Road	Sunningfield	RG12 4GH	01181236576	Ms	B	Masters
6	01-Aug-03	Masterson Taxis	112 New Road	Sunningfield	RG12 4GH	01181236576	Ms	B	Masters
4	02-Jul-03	Express Hire	Station Approach	Cambertown	GU13 5GH	01267377377	Mrs	B	Jones
(AutoNumber)									

Figure 6.9

Tip:

*It is important to select fields like **RegistrationNumber** from **tblFitting**. Always use the field from the 'one' side of a relationship rather than from the 'many' side.*

Now you need to add calculated fields for **CostBeforeDiscount**, **DiscountValue** (if any), **NetCost**, **VAT**, and **TotalCost**. Remember to multiply the **CustomerPrice** by the number of tyres fitted to get the **CostBeforeDiscount**. The other calculations are similar to the ones you did in **qryReminder**.

CostBeforeDiscount: [NumberOfTyres]*[CustomerPrice]

DiscountValue: IIf([Discount],[NumberOfTyres]*[CustomerPrice]*0.05,0)

NetCost: [NumberOfTyres]*[CustomerPrice]-[DiscountValue]

VAT: [NetCost]*0.175

TotalCost: [NetCost]+[VAT] ·

Expression Builder

The **CostBeforeDiscount** field in this query is calculated by multiplying the **NumberOfTyres** by **CustomerPrice**. You can use the **Expression Builder** to enter the formula in the query.

- Return to **Design View**.

- Click in the next free field name cell.

- Click on the **Expression Builder** icon in the toolbar.

The following screen will be displayed:

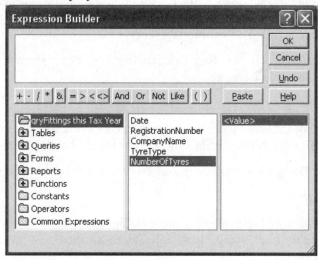

Figure 6.10

- Click on **NumberOfTyres** in the middle column.

- Click the ***** in the operators.

- Double-click on the **+** to expand the **Tables** folder in the left-hand column.

- Click on **tblTyre** in the list of **Tables** (this is why this table had to be added earlier).

- Select **CustomerPrice** and **Paste**.

- Click **OK**.

- Run the query.

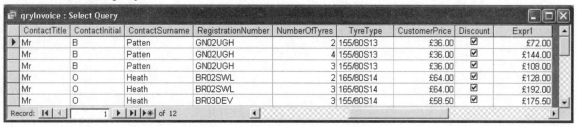

Figure 6.11

The heading of the calculated column is not very helpful. It is easy to rename that.

- Return to **Design View**.

- Place your cursor in the heading of the calculated field and delete **Expr1**.

- Enter *CostBeforeDiscount*.

Parameters

You will be producing invoices daily for different cars, and you need to be able to specify a particular car and date when you run the query to produce just the invoice you want to print. This type of query is called a **Parameter Query**.

- In the criteria cell for **RegistrationNumber**, type *[Enter Registration Number:]*, including the square brackets.

- **Run** the query.

- When prompted, use Figure 6.7 to enter one of the registration numbers that has had more than one fitting. All the fittings for that car should be displayed.

- Return to **Design View** and in the criteria cell for the date, type *[Enter date]*.

- **Run** the query again.

- You will be asked to enter both pieces of information. Enter the registration number and fitting date for a car, using Figure 6.7. The result should be just the one record you need.

- Save your query again.

This query will display the particular car and the date of this fitting. It displays the number and type of tyre, customer price, discount (if any), net cost, VAT and total cost.

Although you can do some of these calculations when you create the invoice report, doing them at the query stage will make producing the final hard copy invoice report easier.

Chapter 7 – Reports

Creating a query for a report

Reports are generated from tables or the results of queries. As an example of a simple report we will create a VAT report for a particular quarter of the year. We need to amend **qryInvoice**, saving it as **qryVAT**, to act as the source of the report.

- In the **Database** window, click the **Query** tab and click **qryInvoice**. Then click **Design**.

- From the **File** menu on the menu bar select **Save As…** and save the new query as *qryVAT*.

- Alter the criterion for **FittingDate** to *Between 01/04/2004 And 30/06/2004*.

- You don't need all the fields to show on the results table which will be the source of the report, so in the **Show** row, deselect all fields except the ones shown in Figure 7.1.

- Delete the criterion for **RegistrationNumber**.

- Run the query. You should see the following data:

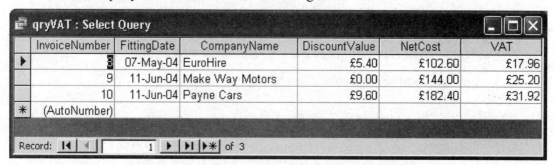

	InvoiceNumber	FittingDate	CompanyName	DiscountValue	NetCost	VAT
▶	8	07-May-04	EuroHire	£5.40	£102.60	£17.96
	9	11-Jun-04	Make Way Motors	£0.00	£144.00	£25.20
	10	11-Jun-04	Payne Cars	£9.60	£182.40	£31.92
＊	(AutoNumber)					

Figure 7.1

- Save your query again and close it to return to the **Database** window.

Creating the report

- In the **Database** window, click the **Reports** tab. Double-click **Create report by using wizard**.

- In the **Report Wizard** window, select **qryVAT** and use the double-headed arrow to select all the fields. Click **Next**.

- We do not need to add any grouping levels, so click **Next**.

- In the next window, select **FittingDate** as the field to sort on. Click **Next**.

- Click **Next** in the next two windows to accept the defaults. Save your report as *rptVAT* and click **Finish**.

Your report will look something like this:

rptVAT

ttingDate	voiceNumber	CompanyName	DiscountValue	NetCost	VAT
07-May-04	8	EuroHire	£5.40	£102.60	£17.96
11-Jun-04	10	Payne Cars	£9.60	£182.40	£31.92
11-Jun-04	9	Make Way Motors	£0.00	£144.00	£25.20

Figure 7.2

Your report needs some editing to make it look neat, and it needs totals at the bottom.

- In **Design View**, drag down the bottom of the **Report Footer** line to give yourself some room in the footer.

- Insert a new field in the Footer section under **NetCost** by clicking the **Text Box** button in the **Toolbox**. Delete the label text by deleting the characters and clicking outside it.

- Delete the text **Unbound** in the **Text** box and replace it with *=Sum(NetCost)*.

- Add another total field under the **VAT** column. You may need to format these fields as **Currency**. To do this, right-click the field and select **Properties**.

- Tidy up the report so that it looks something like this:

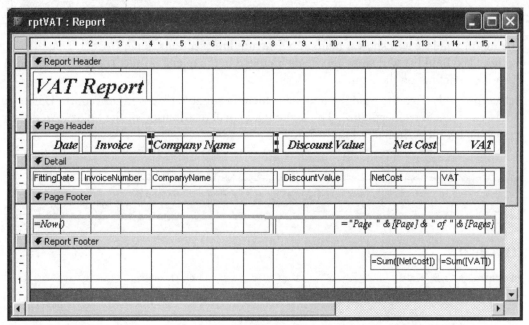

Figure 7.3

- Click the **View** button to see the report. It should look something like this:

VAT Report

Date	Invoice	Company Name	Discount Value	Net Cost	VAT
07-May-04	8	EuroHire	£5.40	£102.60	£17.96
11-Jun-04	10	Payne Cars	£9.60	£182.40	£31.92
11-Jun-04	9	Make Way Motors	£0.00	£144.00	£25.20
				£429.00	£75.08

Figure 7.4

- When you are happy with the report, save and close it.

Creating the invoice

The invoice will be produced as a report. This time, the report will be created in **Design View**.

- From the **Database** window, select **Reports**, and then select **New**.

- Select **Design View**.

- Select the parameter query created for the invoice, **qryInvoice**. This will give easy access to those fields needed in the actual hard copy invoice report. Click **OK**.

Creating the report in Design View

The report window will show a blank report, with three sections, Page Header, Detail and Page Footer. The field list will show the fields included in the query. If the **Toolbox** is not open, open it by clicking on the icon.

Select the fields from the field list and place them in suitable places in the report. Delete any labels you consider superfluous. Think about a logical distribution of the fields. An example of a possible layout is shown in Figure 7.5.

Figure 7.5

- Save the report with the name **rptInvoice** at intervals as you develop it.

Figure 7.6 shows the report in **Design View**.

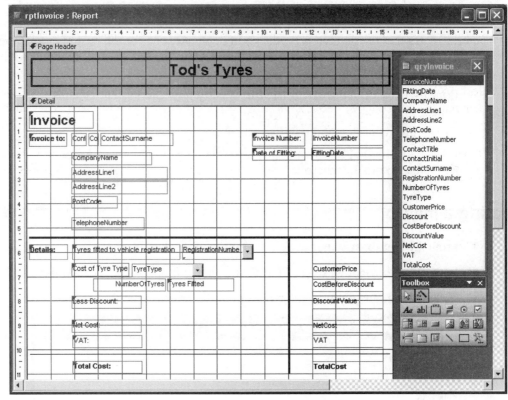

Figure 7.6

Points to note

♦ All the fields specified in your parameter query will be available to the report, because you have identified that query as its source.

♦ Some of the labels have been removed as unnecessary clutter. Remember the different cursor shapes: the open hand for selecting both label and field, and the pointing finger for selecting just one of them.

 ♦ Labels such as **Tod's Tyres** and **Tyre fitting to** are inserted using the label icon, from the **Toolbox**.

 ♦ This icon, a warning from Access, will appear if you insert a label that is not associated with a data item. For this report, you should click on it with the right mouse button and select **Ignore**.

♦ Field alignment has been tidied up. To do this, select the relevant fields together using the **Shift** key. Click the right mouse button and select **Align**, **Left**.

♦ Figure 7.5 is NOT a hard copy of the invoice. It is a screen dump that has been inserted into a text document and would not be accepted as evidence if the examination asks for a hard copy.

Tip:
As long as the invoice is neat and tidy, and includes the necessary information, extra frills will not gain any extra marks. However, a typical question in these exams is about aspects of design that you have considered, so it is useful to have thought about some of these, such as size of font, spacing and layout.

Duplicate copy

The brief states that the invoice is produced in duplicate; one for the customer and one for Tod's records.   This could be achieved in a number of ways; but the chosen method should be stated clearly in the documentation. Here are two suggestions:

– Print two copies. You would need to specify how the system ensures that this is always done.

– Use an impact printer and two-part paper.

We will use a macro to automatically print two copies of the invoice. A button will be placed on a custom toolbar to run the macro.

Creating a macro

- From the **Database** window, select **Macros**, then click **New**.

- In the **Macro** window, select **PrintOut** from the drop-down list of **Actions**.

- In the **Action Arguments** at the bottom of the screen, specify *2* **Copies**.

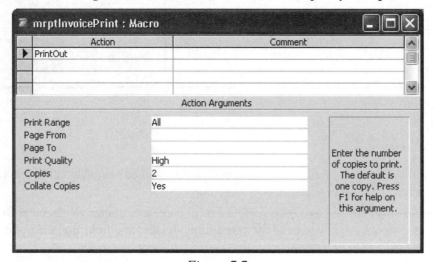

Figure 7.7

- Save the macro as *mrptInvoicePrint*.

- Close the **Macro** window.

Creating a custom toolbar

Now we need a button to run the macro. This will be placed in a custom toolbar.

- From the menu bar select **View**, **Toolbars**, **Customize...**

- Click on the **Toolbars** tab, then click **New**. Call the new toolbar *Tod's Tyres*.

- Go to **Commands**, **Find**, **All Macros**. The name of your new macro will be displayed in the right-hand pane.

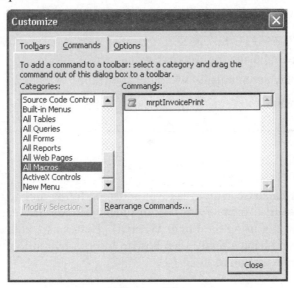

Figure 7.8

- Drag the name onto the new toolbar.

- Right-click to change its properties. You can rename it *Print 2 copies*.

Figure 7.9

- With the invoice in **Print Preview**, test out your new button.

Chapter 8 – The Switchboard

Objectives

By the end of this chapter you will have:

created a front end menu using the Access Switchboard;

made the menu display automatically when the application is loaded;

tested your switchboard.

Menus

When you create a database which has a number of forms and reports, the whole project is improved by the use of a menu form. With older versions of Access, this can be created in Design View (that is, not using the **Form Wizard**). Buttons are added to open forms or reports, or to run queries. You have already seen how to insert a button to close a form, and creating a menu form is just an extension of this.

The switchboard

The later versions of Access have a feature called a **Switchboard Manager**, which simplifies this process even further.

You should first draft your menu structure on paper. Although you could decide to group similar tasks together by adding another level, the menu structure for Tod's system can be quite straightforward, as in Figure 8.1.

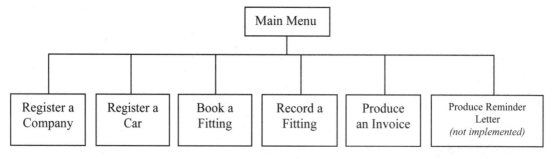

Figure 8.1

Creating the switchboard

- From the **Database** window select **Tools**, **Database Utilities**, **Switchboard Manager**.

- You will get a message saying there is no valid switchboard in the database, would you like to create one – say **Yes**.

- As you are creating a new switchboard, select **New**, call it *Tod's Tyres* and click **OK**.

- Select the page **Tod's Tyres** and click **Edit**.

- To add your first task, click **New**.

- Type in a descriptive name for the first task: *Register a New Company*.

- Choose what task is to be done – here you would want to **Open a form in Add mode**.

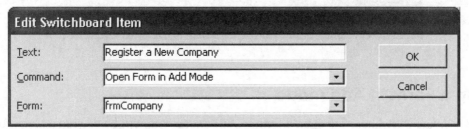

Figure 8.1

- Select **frmCompany** as the form is to be opened. Click **OK**.

- Add the other tasks shown in Table 8.1 to the menu.

Task name	Command	Form
Register a New Car	Open form in Add mode	frmCar
Book a Fitting	Open form in Add mode	frmFitting
Record a Fitting	Open form in Edit mode	frmFitting
Produce an Invoice	Report operation	

Table 8.1

- When all tasks have been entered, select **Close**.

- Now select your switchboard and make it the default, before closing the wizard.

- In the Database window, double-click **Switchboard** to open your menu. It will have the title *Tod* if that is what your database is called.

- Switch to **Design View** and edit the title to *Tod's Tyres*.

- Test all the items in your switchboard.

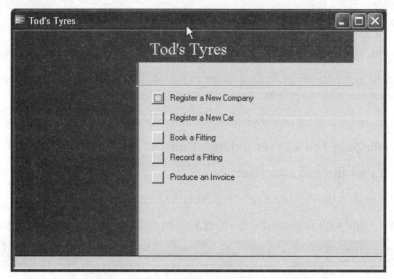

Figure 8.2

Opening a Form in Add mode

When you use your switchboard to open a form in **Add** mode, you will be offered a blank form and *record 1 of 1*. Don't worry! A quick glance at the relevant table will reassure you that any records that you have already entered are safely stored. It is just the first additional record that you are entering.

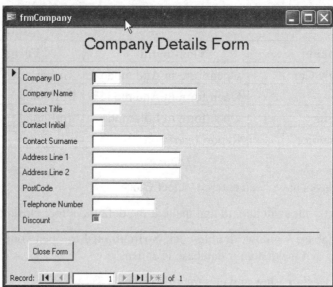

Figure 8.3

- Test all the other items on your menu.

Startup

It is simple to arrange that your database will open with the switchboard, or with any other specified form.

- From the **Database** window, select **Tools, Startup**.

- The following dialogue box will open:

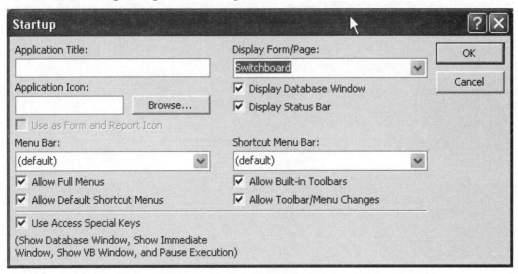

Figure 8.4

- In the **Display Form/Page** box select **Switchboard**.

- Click **OK**.

You can test this by closing your database and reopening it.

You can download sample documentation for this task from the website

www.payne-gallway.co.uk. Then you should be ready to tackle your own project or task!

Part 2

Stages of a Project

In this section:

Chapter 9 – Choosing a Project

Objectives

By the end of this chapter you should:

understand what constitutes a suitable project;

understand the constraints on the choice of hardware and software;

know how to go about choosing your own project;

know how to work out a schedule to meet the project deadline.

Requirements for a computer project

Generally, when a project forms part of a computing course, you will be expected to produce a **complete, well-documented system**. You have to demonstrate that you can solve an information processing problem using the most appropriate means available. Projects should be selected which allow you to demonstrate skills of practical application and problem solving, as well as the techniques of documentation and system testing. Note that for the AQA 'A' Level Computing exam, although it is envisaged that you will develop a complete working solution, *the project report need contain only carefully selected samples of evidence in order to demonstrate each skill.*

You are more likely to develop a successful project if you can find a real user with a real problem to be solved; otherwise the project turns into a textbook exercise with invented problems and unrealistic solutions.

Choice of hardware and software

If you are developing a project for a real user, you may be asked to produce software that will run on the equipment they already own, for example a PC or Apple Macintosh. If this is an exam project rather than something you are doing for payment, you would be well advised to use the hardware and software that you have easy access to, even if the system is never actually implemented for the user. Most users understand the constraints that you are working under and will still be happy to explain their current system and what the requirements of a new system would be. There is always the possibility that you could convert it at a later date if they really want it!

There may be a wide range of software to choose from. If you want to write a complete database application, software such as MS Access may be a good option. A computer-aided design system may be easier to program in C. If you are thinking of computerising the accounts of a small business, a specialised accounting package may be your best choice. But, ultimately, you will have to choose from the software that you or your college or school have, even if the project could be done better or faster another way.

The choice of project

Choosing a project is the first hurdle. It needs to be sufficiently meaty to enable you to gain the maximum possible marks, but not so ambitious that you cannot get it finished in the time available. About 20% of the marks may be awarded for 'Analysis of requirements', which will include finding out how the current system works and what the inputs and outputs are, as well as what the user would like the new system to do. Obviously, it is going to be much easier to get these marks if you have a real user with a real problem to be solved, or a real application which would benefit from computerisation.

By contrast, if for example you choose to create a new computer game, it may be difficult or impossible to fulfil the criteria set by your Examination Board. For example, the AQA specifies that 'candidates should investigate a *real* problem associated with a user whose realistic needs should be taken into account when designing the solution.'

Typically, an 'A' Level Computing or Information Technology candidate is expected to:

♦ analyse a real and realistic problem, identify the requirements of a potential user and identify the parts which are appropriate for a computer solution;

♦ determine the requirements for a computer solution, specify possible solutions and select an appropriate one;

♦ select and apply appropriate techniques and principles to develop algorithms for the solution of problems;

♦ implement algorithms to produce a documented and tested system using, as appropriate, existing or purpose-designed software, and appropriate hardware.

All Boards have somewhat similar standards. You should check the specification for your own Examining Board to make sure your choice of project is appropriate.

Choosing your own project

The most important things to remember when you choose your project are:

♦ Choose something that interests you – after all, you are going to spend the next several months on it. If you are a member of a football club or cricket club, or have a part-time job in a restaurant, shoe shop or sports centre, for example, observe or ask how things are done at present. Organisations such as clubs or societies involve administrative functions which could often benefit from some form of computerisation.

♦ Many ideas which at first seem lacking in scope can be turned into very good projects with a little imagination. Careful work on the user interface, file design and output goes a long way. But be realistic – is it really worth using a computer to keep records of fifteen people in the badminton club who each pay an annual subscription of £5.00?

♦ Whatever your strengths and weaknesses in computing, as soon as you start work on your project you will probably realise you don't know how to tackle part of it. Perhaps you don't know enough about file design, or you would like to use the function keys in a program but don't know how. You may find some of the answers in this book, but very likely you will have to do extra research on your own. Try the library first, and if that has nothing, splash out and buy a good book on Visual Basic, Delphi or Access, or whatever package you intend to use.

♦ If the thought of 'data processing' and updating files bores you, consider other areas of your specification such as compiler-writing, expert systems, simulation, graphics or process control. Again, you will have to do your own research and this will probably cost both time and money, but it could be worth it. Check the requirements of your specification first.

Drawing up a schedule or timetable

Obviously your schedule will depend on the length of time you have available to complete the project. On a two-year 'A' level course, you should probably start thinking of ideas in the summer term of your first year, and start on the analysis in the holidays or immediately you return in September. Spend time doing careful design work for the whole project before you start programming in the second half of the term.

Testing the system and writing up the documentation can take as long as writing the programs, so be sure to leave enough time for this before the deadline. Once you have done the initial design work, you can draw up a detailed schedule of programs or forms, reports, and so on to be designed, coded and tested.

A sample schedule

Task	Start date	Finish date (estimated)
Analysis	Sep 5	Sep 30
Design	Oct 1	Oct 14
Prototype	Oct 15	Nov 14
Further Design	Nov 15	Nov 30
Programming	Dec 1	Jan 31
System testing	Feb 1	Feb 20
User Evaluation	Feb 21	Mar 7
Documentation	Mar 1	Mar 20
Hand in:		Mar 30

Ideas for computer projects

Many good projects involve file handling of some sort. Nearly all these projects will involve storing information on a master file or database, and then querying and updating it. This in itself is not enough to form a project – ask yourself what the *point* of the system is. There is no point putting data *into* a system if you don't get anything *out* of it, so concentrate on what the output will be. Generally speaking, a reasonably substantial project will involve more than one file – perhaps a file of transactions as well as a master file, or two master files linked in some way. A complete database will almost certainly involve several related tables.

These are some ideas for projects which can be implemented in MS Access.

1. **Newsagent's Database**

   Summary: The main objectives of this system are:

   - to make delivery orders easier to implement;
   - to allow newspaper price changes to be made quickly and easily;
   - to allow data retrieval for a specific customer;
   - to print a daily sheet for each paperboy/girl specifying which newspapers are to be delivered to each customer;
   - to make paper orders to suppliers more accurate by calculating exactly the number of newspapers needed;
   - to make a billing system that is both itemised and clear.

   Comment: This is an ambitious project, which could be made more manageable by omitting the billing side, while making provision for this to be programmed at a later date. The newsagent's requirements need careful analysis; for example, how are customers' holidays (when no papers are required) recorded? The current method of recording data needs to be looked at, and suitable report formats agreed with the prospective user. This is a good project for someone with experience as a paperboy/girl or who has worked in a newsagent's shop.

2. **Repair and Cleaning Service Job Control**

   Summary: The project is designed to assist in the smooth running of a business which repairs, cleans and proofs horse rugs. Batches of rugs arrive for this service, and records are kept on customers, batches and individual rugs. The processing of a rug is tracked as it moves from washing to mending to proofing to packing. Invoices are produced by the system.

   Comment: This project could be implemented in Visual Basic linked to an Access database. It involves some complex tasks making good use of objects, parameter passing, iteration and selection. Error handling routines and validation checks should be built in.

3. **Theatre Booking System**

   Summary: The aim of this system is to handle bookings for plays (either for an amateur dramatic society or a local theatre), keeping a database of plays, customers and seats booked. Tickets need to be printed, and management reports may be required showing the attendance for different plays or seasons. Letters may be mailed to selected customers if bookings are slow for a particular show.

   Comment: It is absolutely essential to have a real user here, to get a clear set of objectives rather than making up your own. If you have worked in a theatre booking office or can spend a day observing and asking questions, this could make an interesting project. The main difficulty with any type of booking system is deciding how to display the available seats (or tennis courts, cottages, etc.).

4.   School Administration

Summary: There may well be some parts of your school or college administration that could benefit from computerisation. For example, students enrolled in the 'A' Level programme at XXX College have their name, address and course code held on the central college database. However, the administrator of the 'A' Level programme needs more information about students than is provided by the college database, such as which subjects they are taking and who their personal tutors are. Class lists can then be prepared for the subject tutors, and grades can be recorded when available so that subject teachers can be informed.

Comment: Once again, a real user is required to explain what would be needed from a new computerised system and exactly what output is required.

5.   Stock control

Summary: A database may be used to record all details of stock and stock transactions. Stock reports and reorder reports can be printed out as required.

Comments: Stock control could be implemented for any small organisation with a limited amount of stock. You are not recommended to try and rewrite Tesco's stock control system! It is *essential* to have first-hand knowledge of the business whose stock control you are computerising, and of the problems and objectives to be tackled.

Specimen project described in this section

A single specimen project is used to illustrate all the stages involved in developing and documenting a project.

The project is implemented in MS Access. The use of a prototype to assist in the design of the final system is illustrated, and then used to demonstrate how to write Visual Basic modules to enhance and customise the final product to the user's requirements.

Part 3 shows an example of a complete sample project.

Naturally, you should study carefully the particular set of guidelines you have been given for your particular course and exam board to make sure that your project meets the marking criteria.

Chapter 10 – Analysis

Objectives

By the end of this chapter you will have considered the following points in the analysis of a system:

how to prepare for an interview with the end-user;

points to cover in the interview;

the importance of ascertaining both *quantitative* and *qualitative* objectives;

the use of a data flow diagram;

consideration of possible solutions;

justification of chosen solution;

a possible framework for writing up the analysis.

The investigation

Once you have decided on your project topic, you must make a full investigation of the user's needs. Be aware that, at Advanced Level, examination boards usually stress the need to actually find a *real* user and obtain *real user feedback*. Having a 'potential' user may reduce the project to one of a distinctly hypothetical nature, not able to satisfy any user at all – and scoring only modest marks.

At AS Level, it may be acceptable to investigate a problem which relates to a hypothetical situation with a *proposed* or envisaged user. For a project submitted in the first year of a modular course, your teacher may be able to set you a problem and act as the end-user. Nevertheless, you are strongly advised to find your own end-user; if the same project is done by several students in a class, all of whom hand in a very similar implementation, you are unlikely to get credit for it, even if most of the original ideas were yours.

The exercise of designing a questionnaire, or preparing a list of questions and holding interviews, should be regarded as an important part of the project; it is, in practice, quite impossible to guess what a real user would want from, say, a club membership system or sports hall booking system. A project based on a real user's problem will win hands down every time over one which tries to guess an imaginary user's requirements.

The analysis is concerned with finding out about the *current* system (if there is one), and what the *requirements* are for the new system.

SPECIMEN PROJECT – A. B. FRAMES LTD.

The specimen project shows how an analysis might proceed. You have established that A. B. Frames is a small family business, run by Mr and Mrs Daniels, which specialises in selling pictures and restoring and framing pictures, photographs, tapestries and so on. There is a possibility that part of their business could benefit from computerisation; specifically, to help them keep track of their customers and what particular artists, subjects, etc., each customer is most interested in.

Typically, the owners of a business such as A. B. Frames may be family members or friends of the family, or you may have been put in touch with them by your teacher.

Preparing for an interview

The first step in a project will usually be to plan an interview with the user. Make sure you have a list of questions prepared, and a notebook handy to write down the user's answers.

The involvement of a real user right from the start is a vital ingredient of a good project. You must show evidence of investigative competence in order to earn top marks in the analysis section.

You will find that preparing questions in advance of an interview focuses your attention on what information is needed, and the interview is less likely to end up as a vague chat about possibilities which still leaves a lot of unanswered questions.

If you have used a questionnaire, samples of the responses can be put into an appendix, and a summary included in the analysis section of your report.

A checklist of points to cover in an interview might include the following:

1. objectives — Exactly what is the new system designed to achieve?

2. input — What format does the input take? What input documents are currently used, and what are the data requirements?

3. output — What will be the output from the new system? Is hard copy required? How often? Is there some output from the current system or a similar system that you can look at?

4. processes — What is done, where, when and how? How are the objectives going to be fulfilled in the new system?

5. data — How much is there? Will the master file contain 50, 500 or 5000 records? How often does it change? How often are new records added or deleted? Do these changes come in batches of several at a time, or in ones and twos?

6. exceptions — How are exceptions and errors handled?

7. security — Is security an issue? Should there be limited access to some or all parts of the new system?

8. problems — What are the drawbacks or problems with the current way of doing things?

9. constraints — Are there any constraints on hardware, software, cost, time and so on?

10. suggested solutions — Does the user have a particular solution in mind?

Quick Answer Questions

Suppose that you have decided to take on the task of computerising some or all of A. B. Frames' business.

1. Assume that you have the opportunity to interview the owner, Mrs Daniels. What questions will you ask her?

2. What documents could you ask to look at?

Answers

1. You should go through the checklist of points to make sure they are covered. Obviously, the list of questions is going to be different for different situations, and you may already know quite a lot about the problem that you are going to solve with the aid of a computer, so don't stick slavishly to a formula. As you get answers, different questions will occur to you. Here is a possible list:

   ♦ Can you tell me how you think a computer may be able to help you in the running of your business?

   ♦ Can you show me how customer orders are currently recorded?

   ♦ What output would you hope to get from the current system?

   ♦ How many regular customers do you have?

   ♦ Do you already have a computer?

   ♦ Do you have any particular package in mind for this project?

2. Ask to see, for example:

   ♦ a sample order form;

   ♦ any manual card index of customers;

   ♦ a list of customers produced by the current system.

Results of the interview

The initial interview has elicited the following facts:

Each time a customer comes in to buy something, or to have a painting framed or restored, a job sheet is completed. The customer is given one copy, a second copy is sent to the workshop with the item to be framed or restored, and a third copy is filed. An example is shown in Figure 10.1.

Frequently, a customer will come back several months later and ask, for example, for another tapestry to be framed 'using the same sort of frame as last time'. This means a lengthy search through hundreds of job sheets, and often the relevant one cannot be located.

The owners would also like some means of identifying which customers are interested in particular artists (e.g. dogs, landscapes, portraits), who are their best customers in terms of jobs or amount spent, which customers are business customers, and so on, so that letters can be sent out inviting selected customers to special events, sales or exhibitions.

Mr and Mrs Daniels have recently purchased a PC and the MS Office suite, including MS Access. However they are finding it very hard to learn how to use Access and set up their own database, and have asked for a customised database application to be created. They would like to learn more about Access and Word themselves so that they could, for example, create a new letter to be sent to a selected set of customers.

A.B.Frames Limited

15 Castle Street, Ipswich IP8 5EW
Telephone (01473) 555322

Vat Reg No. 332 990477 32

Order No **4842**

Date Required **5th August**

Customer Name
and Address

W Graham
12 Cranford Drive
Ipswich

Tel No.

Description
of Work

Old dog

Frame **193 Painted Blue**   Size **14 x 17**

Conservation Mount [ ]   Colour **Blush White**

Glass [ ]   Norm [ ]   N/R [ ]   Perspex [ ]

Back [ ]   Norm [ ]   S/U [ ]   Fitting [ ]

SPECIAL INSTRUCTIONS

Paid in Full

Price (inc VAT) £   Deposit Paid £

Figure 10.1: The Job Sheet

Adding in more detail

If the above couple of pages were to be handed in to the AQA as the Project Analysis, it would almost certainly fall into the second category of 'Some analysis but limited in perception and scope. Some evidence of investigation of a problem with limited scope resulting in a standard exercise with few external constraints. Statement of system objectives but lacking in scope and depth. Some evidence of consideration of user requirements.' Mark: 4 out of 12.

To lift this analysis into the next category, you need to consider the problem in more detail. For instance, you could ask the following questions:

♦ What data needs to be held about each customer? (e.g. if the customer is a business customer, should we hold the name and address of their business?)

♦ What are the main objectives of the system?

♦ What data needs to be held about each job? Do we need to hold all the data on the current job sheets?

♦ Is there ever more than one item per job?

♦ Is the intention to enter jobs while the customer is actually at the shop counter, or will the jobs still be entered manually using the old job sheets, and then some of the information transferred later to the database?

♦ Exactly what is the expected output from the system? Are any reports required?

♦ Do we need to design and save queries to find various categories of customer such as 'all business customers', or do the users want to be shown how to make queries themselves?

♦ How much of the Mail Merge operation should be automated?

♦ Would it be a good idea to include an option to delete all customers who have been 'inactive' for, say, the last three years?

♦ Is a password system needed?

♦ Should provision be made for automatically backing up the data?

Detailed analysis

More detailed enquiries about the proposed database revealed the following facts:

Input data

Data needs to be kept for both customers and jobs.

Customer data

The following data needs to be held for each customer:

Name;

Address;

Business customer? (Y/N);

Business name (if a business customer);

Customer interests: Framing/Sales/Restoration/Tapestry/Exhibition? (or any combination of these).

Job data

The current system of manually recording jobs is quite informal, and if a customer wants more than one picture framed, for example, two job sheets may be filled in with the same job number and notes made in the 'Special Instructions' field. **The new computerised system should allow for more than one item per job, for example a sale and a restoration**.

For each job, the following data must be stored:

Job number;

Job date;

Customer name and address;

Type of item: sales, restoration or framing. (n.b. may be more than one different item);

Description;

Type of frame (if framing item);

Artist name and subject matter (if sales);

Job value.

Output

The following reports are required:

♦ a list of all business customers;

♦ a list of all customers whose total jobs exceed a given value;

♦ a list of all customers interested in, for example, a given artist, or given subject matter, or who fall into various categories such as 'Framing', 'Tapestry', 'Sales', 'Exhibition', or 'Restoration'.

The owners would also like the ability to mail letters to selected customers.

Other requirements

An important requirement is that any customer information can be quickly located on screen, including details of all the jobs that the customer has ordered in the past.

It is not intended to replace the current manual method of recording jobs. The jobs will still be recorded in the same way, and then entered into the database once a week. Possibly at a future date the manual system will be completely replaced, but the owners wish to proceed cautiously until they feel more confident with their PC and the Access software.

Comments on this project

This project has to be implemented in MS Access, because that is what the customer has requested. It offers plenty of scope, and can be tackled on a number of levels; the whole system could be implemented using 'wizards', but would it really meet the customer requirements?

In Advanced Level Computing, **examiners are unlikely to award the highest grades to a project which has not involved some programming of either macros or modules, or both.**

One approach is to use the 'wizards' at the Design stage to build a prototype of the final solution, which can be shown to the intended user who may then have some suggestions for other facilities they would like included. The prototype can then either be discarded or developed into the final solution.

It would be a good idea to include some evidence of user involvement at this stage, perhaps getting the user to 'sign off' the final design.

Ascertaining the objectives

The objectives of the proposed new system need to be formally identified and stated. Turn to the sample project in Part 3 to see how they have been written down. You should include both *qualitative* and *quantitative* objectives, bearing in mind that it is bad practice to have any purely qualitative objectives.

An example of a qualitative objective is:

"It should be easy to locate a particular customer invoice".

An example of a quantitative objective is:

"It should be possible to locate any customer invoice in under 30 seconds".

The more clearly your objectives are stated, the easier it will be to evaluate your final solution with reference to the objectives.

General objectives for a system

The objectives for your own project will obviously be different from those for this project.

They may be, for example:

♦ to provide management information of some kind;

♦ to provide a better service to customers, members of a club, or anyone else affected by the new system;

♦ to save time and effort for the person who is currently performing the task manually;

♦ to perform some task better or more accurately than has previously been possible;

♦ to cut costs or save money in some way;

♦ to give enjoyment or entertainment to the user.

These general objectives need to be stated in specific, measurable terms for each individual project.

There are other objectives which are often given by students, but which are of dubious value. For example:

♦ *to create a user friendly system*

Yuk! This is a most overworked phrase. Granted, any system wants to be as easy to use as possible, but it is really not an end in itself. When stated as the first objective, it usually means that the student has not actually thought about what the real objectives are.

♦ *to enable me to learn more about object-oriented programming (or whatever)*

This needs to be a beneficial spin-off rather than the primary purpose of the project. If there isn't a real purpose, perhaps you should think of another project! The objectives will relate to the desired *output* of the system.

Analysis of the system is not something you can do in three-quarters of an hour. You must try to think yourself into the position of the user and understand all the complexities of their task, if you are going to produce something really usable at the end of it all. You will probably keep coming back to your interview notes throughout the project, as problems crop up in the design and development stages. It is very important to keep notes of the preliminary investigation or interview to which you can refer. A summary of the main points of the interview can be included in the Analysis section of the report, but bearing in mind the upper limit on the length of the report, a transcript is **not** required.

Drawing a data flow diagram

A data flow diagram is often a good way of summarising the sources and destinations of data, and the processing that takes place. It shows how data moves through a system and what data stores are used. It does not specify what type of data storage is used or how the data is stored.

A data flow diagram for the specimen project is shown in Part 3.

The following four symbols are used in data flow diagrams:

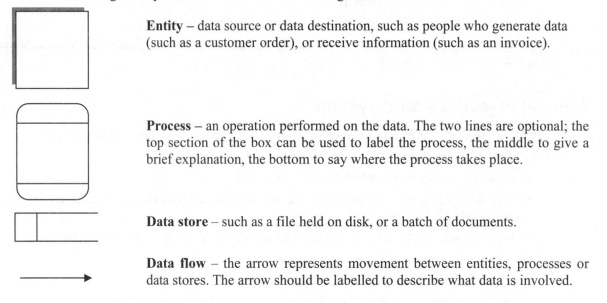

Entity – data source or data destination, such as people who generate data (such as a customer order), or receive information (such as an invoice).

Process – an operation performed on the data. The two lines are optional; the top section of the box can be used to label the process, the middle to give a brief explanation, the bottom to say where the process takes place.

Data store – such as a file held on disk, or a batch of documents.

Data flow – the arrow represents movement between entities, processes or data stores. The arrow should be labelled to describe what data is involved.

Consideration of possible solutions

You need to consider carefully how the objectives will be best achieved. Should you use a package, or write a suite of programs? What programming language would be most suitable? Is that language available for you to use, or are you constrained by the software which you or the end-user has access to? Are there any constraints on hardware? Are you sure that a computerised solution is really the best one, or would it be preferable to improve the manual methods? (If so, think of another project!)

The most important person to consider is the end-user – in the case of the specimen project, the owner of the business. If she has a PC and wants to use Access, then your choices are pretty limited. Even so, you should at least write a justification of your chosen method of solution if this is required by your Board's specification. (Note that 'consideration of possible solutions' is not required by the AQA 'A' Level Computing specification.)

Proposed solution

Your proposed solution, describing the software and hardware you intend to use, should be stated and justified. You may be able to justify your choice on the grounds of what facilities a particular language or package has that will make your job easier.

The trend in the past few years is for more and more students to choose to use a software package for their projects rather than writing a suite of programs. As the facilities offered by the various packages are generally quite easy to learn to use, and packages are becoming both cheaper and more powerful, this approach makes a good deal of sense and you should give it serious consideration. The implementation will probably be very much quicker, allowing you more time for thorough testing and documentation, both important aspects of a project. But remember that for an 'A' Level project, you will be expected to do some programming of macros or modules even if you are using a software package.

Writing up the analysis

A possible framework for writing up the analysis is given below:

1. **Introduction**
   1.1 Background
   1.2 Identification of the prospective user
2. **Investigation**
   2.1 The current system (including summary of main points of interview if appropriate)
   2.2 Data flow diagram
   2.3 Data sources and destinations
   2.3 Problems with the current system
3. **Objectives of the new system**
   3.1 General objectives
   3.2....3.n Specific objectives
4. **Constraints**
   4.1 Hardware
   4.2 Software
       4.3 Time (including a well-defined schedule of activities)
       4.4 User's knowledge of Information Technology
5. **Limitations of the new system**
   5.1 Areas which will not be included in computerisation
   5.2 Areas considered for future computerisation
6. **Proposed solution**
   6.1 Realistic appraisal of the feasibility of potential solutions
   6.2 Justification of chosen solution
   6.3 E-R Models if appropriate
   6.4 Identification of objects, and object analysis diagrams, if appropriate

Of course, not every analysis will fit the model precisely! It is merely intended as a starting point from which you may diverge.

Before you continue any further

When you have written up the analysis, you should hand it in to your project supervisor (teacher or lecturer) to check that the proposals provide scope for sufficient range and depth to be a worthwhile AS or A Level project. If it isn't, it's better to face the truth sooner rather than later!

Your teacher should also be able to spot whether you have chosen a project that is too ambitious and is unlikely to be completed before the deadline. If that is the case, it should be possible to limit the project to a well-defined part of a larger system.

Chapter 11 – Design

Objectives

By the end of this chapter you will have covered the following points in the design of a system:
overall system design;

producing a conceptual model;

drawing an entity-relationship diagram;

analysis of data requirements;

input content and format;

data validation;

output;

user interface design;

charts showing overall systems design;

program or module specification(s);

security and backup;

design of test strategy.

Take time over design

The Design stage is a crucial part of any project, since a poor design will almost certainly mean that the project will not be successfully implemented. Programming should not start until the design is completed. Someone once made the point that the design stage is often rushed in order to allow time at the end of the project to correct the mistakes that were caused by rushing the design stage...

Overall system design

In this section you should describe briefly the inputs, processing and outputs that make up the system. A *system outline chart* (see specimen project in Part 3) is a convenient way of showing these. A *systems flow chart* shows similar information, but also shows the sequence of events.

Producing a conceptual model

From the statement of requirements, a conceptual data model can be produced. This will show the entities, attributes and relationships.

♦ An *entity* is a thing of interest to the business; for example *customer*, or *job*.

♦ An *attribute* is a property or characteristic of an entity, such as *customer name*, *address*, or *job number*.

♦ A *relationship* is a link or association between entities. For example there is a one-to-many relationship between *customer* and *job*.

The entities in the A. B. Frames application are CUSTOMER, JOB, and ITEM. You should show the relationships between the entities by drawing an *entity relationship diagram*:

Figure 11.1: Entity relationship diagram

Input content, format and validation

Once you have produced a data model like the one above, you can start to design the structure of the database. Make sure the tables are correctly structured from your entity-relationship diagram, and then write down the attributes in each table, identify the primary key, and decide on any validations and default values that can be attached to any field.

The tables for A. B. Frames are defined as follows:

CUSTOMER   (Table name: **tblCustomer**)

Attribute Name	Data Type	Max Length	Default value	Description/ Validation
CustomerID*	Long Integer			Unique primary key
Title	Text	4	Mr	
Surname	Text	25		Mandatory[1]
Initials	Text	3		Must be uppercase
Street	Text	30		
Village	Text	30		
Town	Text	30		
County	Text	20	Suffolk	
PostCode	Text	10		Must be uppercase
HomeTelephone	Text	15		
WorkTelephone	Text	20		
SalesCustomer	Yes/No		No	
FramingCustomer	Yes/No		No	

[1] In terms of Access properties, set **Required** to *Yes*, and **Allow Zero Length** to *No*.

RestorationCustomer	Yes/No		No	
TapestryCustomer	Yes/No		No	
ExhibitionCustomer	Yes/No		No	
BusinessCustomer	Yes/No		No	Must be Yes if BusinessName not empty
BusinessName	Text	30		
CustomerNotes	Memo			

*Table 11.1: The **tblCustomer** table*

JOB   (Table name: **tblJob**)

Attribute Name	Data Type	Max. Length	Default value	Description/ Validation
JobNo*	Long Integer			Unique primary key
CustomerID	Long Integer			Must exist on Customer table
Orderdate	Date			
JobValue	Currency			Calculated field (total of individual item values)
ItemsInJob	Integer		1	The number of items on this job sheet
JobNotes	Memo			

*Table 11.2: The **tblJob** table*

ITEM   (Table name: **tblItem**)

Attribute Name	Data Type	Max. Length	Default value	Description/ Validation
ItemNo*	Integer		1	Must be numeric (ItemNo and JobNo constitute the unique primary key)
JobNo*	Long Integer			Must exist on tblJob table
ItemType	Text	11		Must be one or more of Sales, Framing, Exhibition, Tapestry or Restoration
ArtistName	Text	20		Only entered if Sale or Exhibition customer
SubjectMatter	Text	20		Description of painting sold, e.g. Dogs, Landscape
ItemValue	Currency			Price charged for Sale/Job
ItemDescription	Text	30		
Frame	Text	20		Type and/or colour of frame

*Table 11.3: The **tblItem** table*

Naming conventions

There are various conventions for naming the objects that you use. You don't have to use a naming convention but it will certainly make your database easier to create and maintain, and could earn you extra marks in project work. Shown on the next page are the Leszynski/Reddick naming conventions, which will be used in this book.

Level 1

Object	Tag	Example
Table	tbl	tblCustomer
Query	qry	qryClientName
Form	frm	frmCustomer
Report	rpt	rptSales
Macro	mcr	mcrUpdateList
Module	bas	basIsNotLoaded

Level 2

Object	Tag	Example
Table	tbl	tblCustomer
Table (lookup)	tlkp	tlkpRegion
Table (system)	zstbl	zstblUser
Query (select)	qry	qryClientName
Query (append)	qapp	qappNewPhone
Query (crosstab)	qxtb	qxtbYearSales
Query (delete)	qdel	qdelOldCases
Query (form filter)	qflt	qfltAlphaList
Query (lookup)	qlkp	qlkpSalary
Query (make table)	qmak	qmakSaleTo
Query (system)	zsqry	zsqryMacroName
Query (update)	qupd	qupdDiscount
Form	frm	frmCustomer
Form (dialogue)	fdlg	fdlgInputDate
Form (menu)	fmnu	fmnuMain
Form (message)	fmsg	fmsgCheckDate
Form (subform)	fsub	fsubInvoice
Report	rpt	rptTotals
Report (subreport)	rsub	rsubValues
Report (system)	zsrpt	zsrptMacroName
Macro	mcr	mcrUpdateList
Macro (for form)	m[formname]	m[formname]Customer
Macro (menu)	mmnu	mmnuStartForm
Macro (for report)	m[rptname]	m[rptname]Totals
Macro (system)	zsmcr	zsmcrLoadLookUp
Module	bas	basTimeScreen
Module (system)	zsbas	zsbasAPIcall

Table 11.4: Leszynski/Reddick naming conventions

Data validation

Any item of data that will be input by the user will be prone to error. As far as possible, you want to make sure that the program will not 'crash' (terminate unexpectedly), whatever the user enters.

In addition, various checks of specific fields can be made, such as range checks, checks for particular characters (e.g. Y or N), checks that a particular record exists, and so on. You have to try and anticipate all the errors that users might make, and either prevent users from making them or provide a way to correct the error before the computer accepts the data.

Data validation is an important aspect of your project, and will earn you extra marks if it is carefully planned and explained. In your report, discuss the reasons for the validations you have chosen.

Checklist of facts to record about each data item

◆ name (note that while Access refers to 'field names', in database terminology fields are referred to as 'attributes');

◆ data type – e.g. alphanumeric, integer, real, or logical (Boolean);

◆ length (if text);

◆ default value;

◆ plain language description;

◆ validation checks.

Output

Referring back to the analysis, the following output is to be produced:

1. **List of Business customers.**

   The fields to be included are Customer Name and Address, Name of Business.

2. **List of customers interested in a particular artist or subject.**

   The fields to be included are Customer Name and Address.

3. **List of customers whose total jobs exceed a given value.**

   The user will enter a value, e.g. £100, and the report will produce a list of all customers whose total jobs exceed this amount. The fields to be included are Customer Name and Address, and Total Job Value.

4. **A mail merge facility to send letters to selected customers.**

5. **Mailing labels.**

   Rather than designing each report manually using pencil and paper, it may be quicker to prototype a solution and include screenshots of each report layout. Then annotate this to show what changes you need to make to get the report into its final form.

The user interface

Data entry screens

If you are using MS Access, 'wizards' may be used for the initial screen creation, and the screens customised so that they look attractive and are easy to use. As most people design screens in this way rather than with paper and pencil, it is acceptable to include a sample prototype screenshot in the Design section, annotated to show your design rationale, and with proposed alterations and extra features sketched in by hand. Do *not* simply include screenshots of your screens in their final implemented form. Take the screenshots early on while you are in the prototyping stage and annotate by hand with your design ideas before proceeding to implement them. It may be wise to save your prototype screens under different names so that you can print a new screenshot whenever you need one.

Tip:

*In Windows, pressing **Alt** and **Print Screen** together will place a copy of the active window in the Clipboard, from where it may be pasted into a Word document or into a graphics program for editing. Pressing **Print Screen** alone captures the entire screen. Alternatively, you can use one of the many screen capture utility programs available.*

Guidelines for screen design

There are many good books written on the subject of screen design, but a few commonsense rules will go a long way:

- ◆ Be sensible in your use of colour. Dark blue text on a black background is almost illegible, yellow on green is merely unpleasant.

- ◆ Use both uppercase and lowercase. All-uppercase sentences are harder to read, and less attractive.

- ◆ Be consistent in your terminology: for example on menu screens, use *Q for 'Quit'* on every menu, not *E for 'Exit'* on some, and *5. Return to main menu* on others.

- ◆ Don't use obscure error messages such as '*Error X551*'. Where possible, replace built-in system error messages with your own more descriptive messages.

- ◆ Help the user wherever possible. For example, the instruction 'Enter date' with no clue as to the correct format, may leave the user floundering. Give an on-screen example of the required format, such as *dd/mm/yy*.

Menu structures

Most projects will probably start by displaying a menu of options from which the user may choose, and some of these choices may lead to submenus. Use the following guidelines when designing your menus:

- ◆ Each menu should be given a title which uniquely identifies it, such as '*Main Menu*', '*Reports Menu*' and so on.

- ◆ The heading on each submenu should display the choice that was made on the previous menu, so that the user always has a clear idea of what option is currently operative. For example, if the user selects **Reports Menu** from the main menu, the next menu should be headed '*Reports Menu*'.

- ◆ The last option on each menu should take the user back to the previous level of menu.

When you have decided on your menu structure, you should draw up an outline chart showing movement between menus, and include this in your project report. An example is given below.

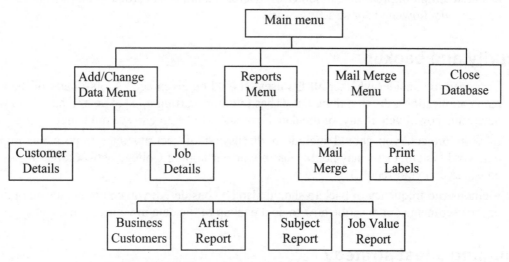

Figure 11.2: Chart showing movement between menus

Charts showing overall systems design

This refers to systems flowcharts, system outline charts or other types of system chart, *not* program flowcharts.

The NCC (National Computing Centre) suggests using the following symbols in systems flowcharts:

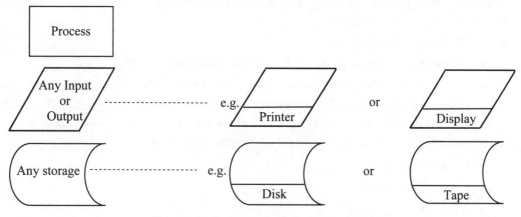

Figure 11.3: Systems flowchart symbols

A systems flowchart and system outline chart for the specimen project is given in Part 3.

Module design and specification

Detailed design of programs, modules or macros should be specified in this section, using pseudocode, flowcharts or structure charts.

Security and backup

You need to consider whether all the users should be given access to all parts of the system. In many applications, the first thing a user has to do on starting up is to enter a password which will determine how much, if any, of the data he or she will be able to see or change.

In your project, you should include a discussion of security and, if possible, implement a password system. (This may not be possible on a school or College network, but it should still be considered in your report.)

Methods and frequency of backup should also be considered; you could include an option on one of the user menus, or describe how to do a backup of the data in your user manual.

Designing a test strategy

It may seem strange to start thinking about testing before you have even started coding, but in fact it is an essential task if everything is going to work correctly once it is installed. You must also take into account that your test file may have only 10 or 20 records, whereas the real file may have several thousand records. Will the system still work?

You will not be expected to enter more than a maximum of 50 records of test data. Examiners do not want you to waste your limited time typing in hundreds of data records for test purposes.

The overall test *strategy* belongs in the Design section of your report. The actual test plan and test data should go in the Testing section. The discussion of how to design a test plan and test data has been put in Chapter 18.

The objectives of testing are:

♦ To ensure the system works correctly under all circumstances;

♦ To ensure that all systems perform all the functions listed in the original specification.

At all stages of testing, there should be a positive attempt to *provoke* system failure, not to avoid it. (Remember, a successful test is one which uncovers a hitherto undiscovered error.)

A test strategy needs to include different types of testing, such as:

♦ Logical testing;

♦ Functional testing;

♦ System testing;

♦ Recovery testing;

♦ User acceptance testing.

These are explained in more detail below.

Logical testing

This involves designing test data to test every path in the system at least once. For a project implemented in Access, this could include the following:

♦ As each input form is completed, every field is tested with both valid and invalid data. Particular attention is paid to validation procedures, default values, tab order and any special features.

♦ Accepted data is stored in the database for use in queries and reports.

♦ Each macro and code module is tested as soon as it is written, using sufficient data to ensure that all statements have been tested at least once.

♦ Sufficient data is added to test all aspects of queries and reports, including any 'exception' cases such as '*No matching records found*' in a query.

♦ Sufficient data is added to ensure that some reports are more than one page in length, to ensure that the page layout on the second page is satisfactory.

♦ Reports are created specifically to provide hard copy of test data used, so that the *expected* results of queries and calculations can be compared with the *actual* results.

♦ All menus, password routines and exits from the program are tested.

♦ When bugs are discovered and/or changes are made, the object (e.g. form, query, report) is tested again with valid and invalid data, bearing in mind that a change in one place sometimes has an unexpected effect in another area of the program.

Functional testing

The purpose of functional testing is to ensure that the program performs all the functions that were originally specified, that all the input is correctly accepted, that output is correctly produced, and that files or tables correctly updated. It relates to the whole system and does not require a technical understanding of the system.

♦ All the functions of the system as originally specified are systematically tested to ensure that nothing has been accidentally omitted or misinterpreted.

♦ A positive attempt is made to anticipate errors that an inexperienced user might make, and tests are made to check the effect of such errors and ensure that they do not result in incorrect actions or bad data being stored in the database.

System testing

♦ On completion of the whole system, each aspect of it is retested to ensure no errors have been introduced.

♦ The system is tested with a realistic amount of data; although you are not expected to spend days typing in hundreds of records, you should test the system with about 50 records in each of the main tables.

Recovery testing

♦ *Recovery testing* can be carried out to determine what happens if, for example, there is a power cut in the middle of data entry. (Is the whole database corrupted? If so, you'd better warn the user to make frequent backups!)

Acceptance testing

♦ The user is invited to test the system to ensure that it fulfills the stated objectives. (If possible, observe this testing, but do not stop the user from making mistakes – your system should cope with unexpected user behaviour!)

Chapter 12 – Prototyping

Objectives

By the end of this chapter you will have:

created tables;

defined relationships;

created input forms;

created reports;

performed a mail merge to selected customers;

created mailing labels;

implemented a menu structure;

built a prototype solution for the specimen project.

Why prototype?

Using MS Access, it does not take very long to create all the tables, input forms, menus and reports needed for the final system. You may decide not to spend any more time on the implementation, other than changing a few colours, headings, and field labels, and hand in the project without doing any further customisation. However, be warned that without doing some programming of modules or macros, it will be almost impossible to get a good grade at A Level.

Once you have built a prototype, it may be obvious what improvements could be made, and most of these will probably involve some programming, even if it is just to calculate a few totals, maximise an input form, or automatically increment a Customer ID. It will be well worth learning how to write modules in Visual Basic, to turn your project into a really usable system.

Building a prototype for the specimen project

In this chapter you will be taken through the steps to create the required tables, relationships, input forms, reports and menus. It is assumed that you have some familiarity with the basics in MS Access. The prototype was built using Access 2003 on Windows XP, but the steps are similar using Access 2000.

Creating a new database

- Open a new blank database in Access.

- Select a suitable folder for your database.

- Enter the filename (e.g. *ABFrames*) in the **File Name** box.

Creating the database tables

Step 1: Creating the tblCustomer table

- In the main database window, the action **Create table in Design view** should be selected. Double-click it, or press **Enter**. (In Access 2000, you will need to click the **Tables**, **New**, select **Design View**, and click **OK**.)

- Define fields as shown below in Figure 12.1. Note that **CustomerID** has been given a type **Number**, and in the **Field Size** parameter in the lower half of the screen, it is defined as **Long Integer**. Refer back to Table 11.1 to give the text fields the correct length.

- Put the cursor in the **Title** field, and then move it to the **Default Value** property in the bottom half of the screen. Enter *"Mr"* (include the quotation marks.)

- Similarly, set the default value of the **County** field to *"Suffolk"*.

- Define **CustomerID** as the key field by highlighting the row and selecting the **Key** icon on the toolbar.

- All of the **Text** fields should have the **Allow Zero Length** property set to **No**.

- Save the table as *tblCustomer*.

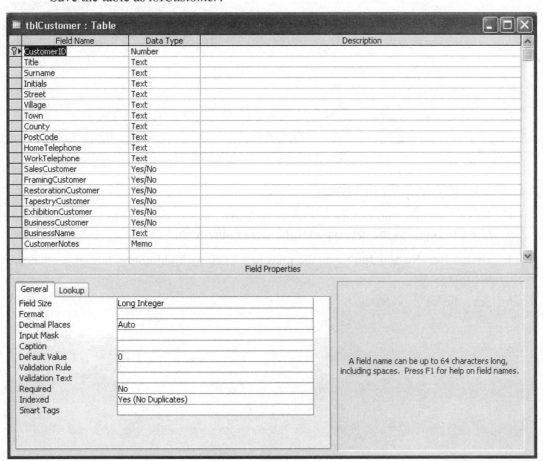

*Figure 12.1: The **tblCustomer** table*

Step 2: Creating the tblJob table

- Follow the same procedure to create the **tblJob** table (Table 11.2 and Figure 12.2). Be sure to use the correct data types for each field, e.g. **Short Date** for the **OrderDate** field, **Memo** for the **JobNotes** field, and **Integer** for the **ItemsInJob** field.

- Define **JobNo** as the primary key, and save the table as *tblJob*.

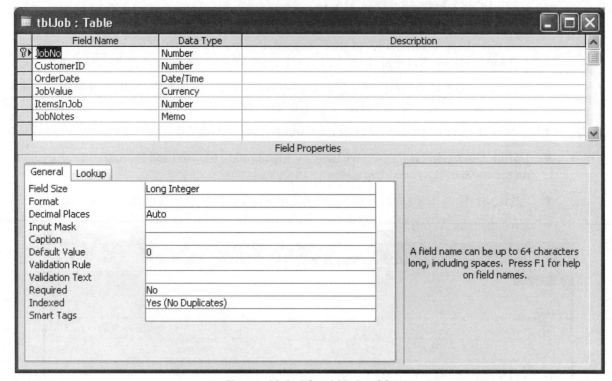

*Figure 12.2: The **tblJob** table*

Step 3: Creating the tblItem table

- Follow the same procedure to create the **tblItem** table (see Table 11.3 and Figure 12.3). Use **Currency** as the data type for the **ItemValue** field.

- Define **ItemNo** and **JobNo** as the joint key field, by highlighting both rows and selecting the **Key** icon.

- Save the table as *tblItem*.

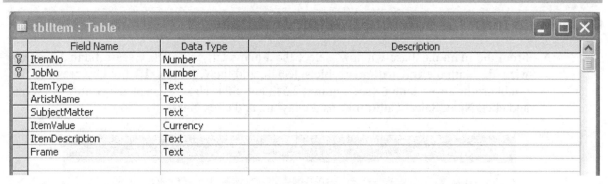

*Figure 12.3: The **tblItem** table*

Defining relationships between tables

- With all the tables closed, click on the **Relationships** tool in the toolbar.

- Add the tables **tblCustomer**, **tblJob** and **tblItem** in that order, and click **Close**. The tables appear in the **Relationships** window; if you have added them in a different order, drag them until they appear as in Figure 12.4.

- Create a one-to-many relationship between **tblCustomer** and **tblJob** by dragging **CustomerID** from **tblCustomer** onto **CustomerID** in **tblJob**.

- (N.B. Always drag from the **one** to the **many** side of the relationship – i.e. *one* customer has *many* jobs.)

- Check **Enforce Referential Integrity** to ensure that it is impossible to enter an item for a non-existent job, and check **Cascade Delete Related Records** to ensure that if you delete a job, all items for that job will automatically be deleted. Click the **Create** button.

- Create a one-to-many relationship between **tblJob** and **tblItem** by dragging **JobNo** from **tblJob** onto **JobNo** in **tblItem**.

- Again, check **Enforce Referential Integrity** and **Cascade Delete Related Records**. Click the **Create** button.

- Close the **Relationships** window, making sure the relationships are saved.

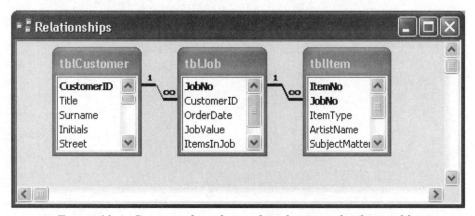

Figure 12.4: Creating the relationships between the three tables

Creating a form for entering Customer details

- From the main database window, select the **Forms** tab and click **Create form by using wizard**. With the **tblCustomer** table selected, add the **CustomerID** field by pressing the double-right-arrow button (see Figure 12.5), and click **Next**. Accept the **Standard** style, and click **Next**. Select **Columnar** as the layout, and click **Next**.

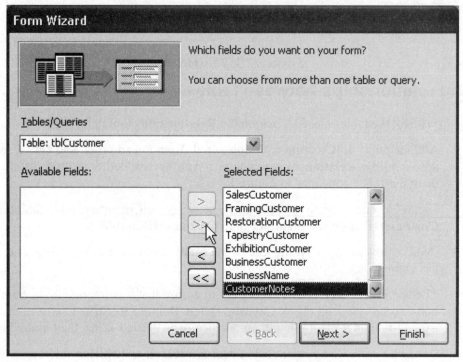

*Figure 12.5: Creating the **frmCustomer** input form*

- Name the form *frmCustomer*, and click **Finish**. It will appear something like the one shown in Figure 12.6.

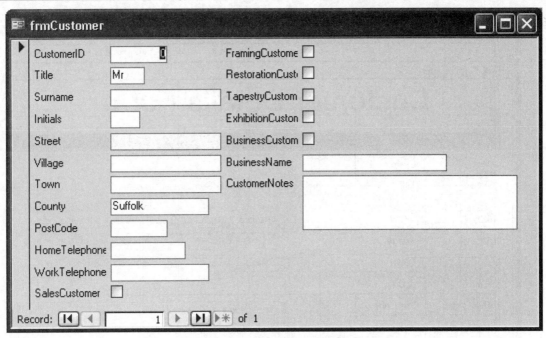

*Figure 12.6: The **frmCustomer** form*

- Switch to **Design View** by clicking the **Design View** icon.

- Create space in the header area by dragging the **Form Header** line downwards.

- Place a text box by clicking the **Label** icon, and then clicking and dragging where the heading **Customer Details Form** is to appear. (Windows 98 Hint: if the **Toolbox** toolbar disappears, try clicking the **frmCustomer** tab at the bottom of the screen).

- Type the text *Customer Details Form*. You can alter its size, justification and font if you like.

- Rearrange the fields on the form by dragging them, so that the form looks something like the one shown in Figure 12.7.

- Save and close the form.

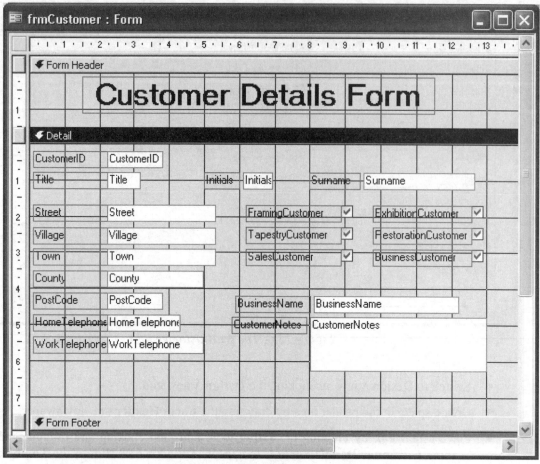

*Figure 12.7: Tailored **frmCustomer** form in design view*

Creating a form for entering Job details

Before you start this form, look back at Figure 10.1 to see what the job sheet looks like in the current manual system. The owners have specified that they do not want all these details on the new computerised job sheet, because they will still be writing out job orders manually and transferring the information to the computer about once a week. The data required on each job is:

> Job number and order date;
> Customer name and address;
> Number of items in the job;
> Total value of the job.

and for each item in a particular job:

> Type of item (sales, restoration, framing etc.);
> Item value;
> Type of frame (if framing item);
> Artist name and subject matter (if sales).

Step 1: Creating a query to combine data from two tables

The data comes from three different tables: **tblCustomer**, **tblJob**, and **tblItem**. The first step is to create and save a query that will combine fields from **tblCustomer** and **tblJob**. The main form will use the resulting table as the source for the main form. That way, as soon as you enter the **CustomerID** for an existing customer, the name and address will be displayed automatically. The items for each job will be entered and listed on a subform.

- From the database window, click the **Queries** tab and select **Create query in Design view**.

- In the **Show Table** dialogue box, add **tblCustomer** and **tblJob**, and then close the dialogue box.

- Place the following three sets of fields in the table shown at the bottom of the screen (see Figure 12.8) by either double-clicking or dragging them, in the following order:

tblJob:	JobNo, OrderDate, CustomerID
tblCustomer:	Title, Initials, Surname, Street, Village, Town, County, Postcode
tblJob:	JobValue, ItemsInJob, JobNotes

  (If the row showing the table names is not visible, select **View**, **Table Names** from the menu.)

- Save the query, giving it the name *qryCustomerJob*, and then close it.

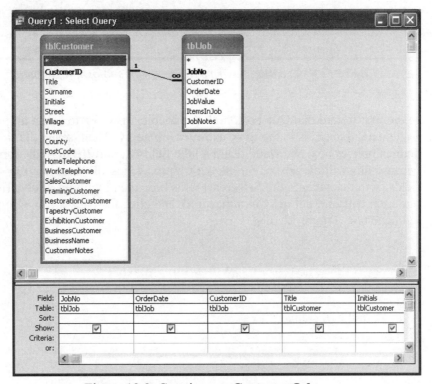

Figure 12.8: Creating **qryCustomerJob**

Step 2: Creating a form with a subform

- As each job may consist of several items, the data entry form for jobs will contain a subform listing each item. Select **Forms**, **Create form by using wizard** from the database window.

- In the **Tables/Queries** list box select **qryCustomerJob**.

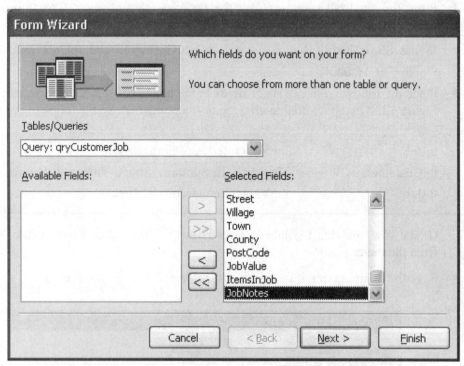

Figure 12.9: Creating the frmJobSheet with subform for Items

- In the first wizard dialogue box, click the double arrow >> to select all the fields from the list of available fields in the **qryCustomerJob** query. Then, select the **tblItem** table in the **Table/Queries** box. We want to add all the fields from **tblItem** to the form except **JobNo**, because this will already be on the main form. Click the double arrow >> to add all the fields from this table to the **Selected Fields** box, then highlight **JobNo** (make sure it's the one from **tblItem**, not **qryCustomerJob)**, and click the back arrow < to put it back in the left hand box (Figure 12.10).

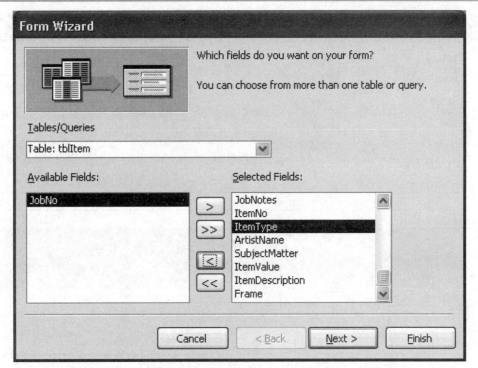

Figure 12.10: Selecting fields for inclusion on the Job sheet

- Click **Next**, and if you have set up the relationships correctly before starting this step, the wizard asks you how you want to view your data. Select **by qryCustomerJob**. On the same page, select the **Form with subform(s)** option. Click **Next**.

- Select **Datasheet** for the layout of the subform. Click **Next**.

- Select the **Standard** style, and click **Next**.

- Give your form the title *frmJobSheet*, and the subform the title *fsubItems*. Click **Finish**; Microsoft Access creates two forms, one for the main form and one for the subform.

The form should look much like the one shown in Figure 12.11.

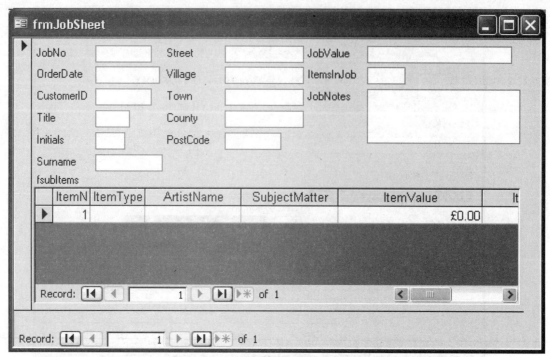

*Figure 12.11: The **frmJobSheet** data entry form*

Testing the data entry forms

You can start work on your test plan at this stage, although you will need to work it out in more detail later on. You should try entering *invalid* as well as valid data. What happens when you try to enter a customer with an ID that already exists on file, or a non-numeric customer ID?

1. Enter about 6 customers, with **CustomerID**s 1 to 6, using the **frmCustomer** data entry form.

    Be sure to include some in each category (sales, framing, etc.) A customer may belong to more than one category.

2. Open the **frmJobSheet** data entry form and enter one or two jobs each for at least three customers, using job numbers starting at 101. Some jobs should contain two or three items – for example a restoration and a framing.

Again, note what happens when you try to enter a job for a non-existent customer, a duplicate job number, or an invalid date.

Start making notes about the weaknesses of these forms. For example:

♦   the job total and number of items in job should be calculated and entered automatically.

♦   how will you find all the jobs for one customer (one of the user's stated requirements)?

♦   when a job is to be entered, how will you be able to find out whether the customer is already on file and, if so, what his/her ID is?

Creating and saving queries to select different categories of customer

Step 1: Creating the query to select all business customers

- From the database window, select **Queries**, **Create query in Design view**.

- In the **Show Table** dialogue box, select **tblCustomer** and click **Add** and then **Close**.

- Double-click each of the fields from **CustomerID** down to **WorkTelephone**, plus the **BusinessCustomer** field, to select them.

- Set the criteria for **BusinessCustomer** to *Yes*. You can deselect **Show**, since this field will simply be *Yes* for all the selected customers.

- Set the **Sort** criteria to **Ascending** on **Surname** and **Initials** to show the customers in alphabetical order of surname and initials.

- Run the query to make sure it works properly, and then save it as *qryBusinessCustomer*.

Step 2: Creating the queries to select customers interested in a particular artist, etc.

For the prototype, it is sufficient to show how one query is created. The other queries will be added in the final version.

Creating a report that lists all business customers

- From the database window, select **Report**, **Create report by using wizard**.

- In the **Report Wizard**, select **qryBusinessCustomer** as the query where the object's data comes from, and click the double arrow >> to select all the fields from the list of available fields. Click **Next**.

- We won't use any grouping levels, so click **Next**.

- The results of the query are already sorted, so no additional sort order is needed; click **Next**.

- Select **Tabular** layout, and click **Next**.

- Select **Soft Gray** as the style, and click **Next**.

- Give the report a title of *rptBusinessCustomer*. Click **Finish**.

- The wizard automatically creates the report, which looks like Figure 12.12.

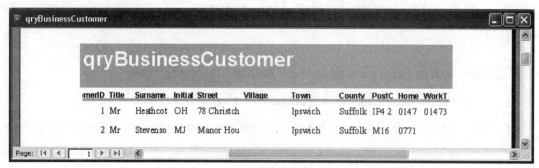

Figure 12.12: The rptBusinessCustomer report

- The report needs tidying up. Switch to **Design View** and see if you can get it to look more like the report shown in Figure 12.13.

- Save it when you have finished.

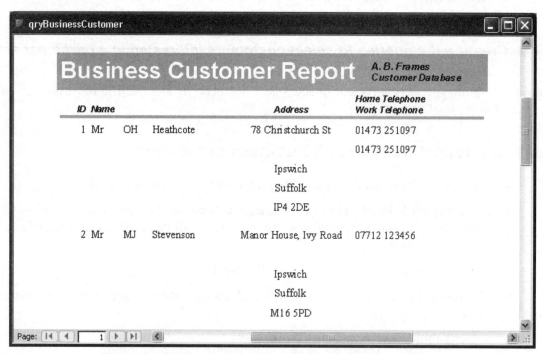

*Figure 12.13: The final version of the **rptBusinessCustomer** report*

Creating mailing labels for all business customers

- From the database window, select **Reports**, and click the **New** icon.

- In the **New Report** dialogue box, select **qryBusinessCustomer** as the query where the object's data comes from, and double-click **Label Wizard**.

- In the **Label Wizard** dialogue box, specify the dimensions of your label. Accept the default settings, or change them if you wish to experiment. Click **Next**.

- In the next dialogue box, select a font and font size (10 or 12 is suitable).

- In the next dialogue box, construct your label as shown in Figure 12.14. Note that there are spaces between the first three fields.

- Continue through the remaining dialogue boxes, saving your label report as *rptBusinessCustomerLabels*. You will then be able to preview your labels on screen.

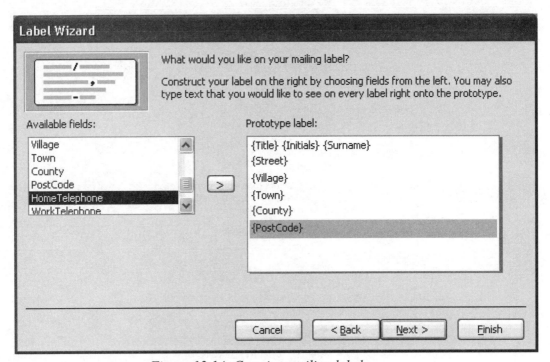

Figure 12.14: Creating mailing labels

Creating a mail merge letter

The standard letter that will be mailed to all selected customers has to be created in Word. This can be done in either of two ways; by opening Word, and then specifying the data source in your Access database (e.g. **qryBusinessCustomer**), or by first specifying the source and then using the OfficeLinks option in Access to open Word automatically. We'll do that now.

- From the database window, click the **Queries** tab and click **qryBusinessCustomer** to select it. This will be the source of names and addresses for the mail merge.

- Press the arrow to the right of the **OfficeLinks** tool. From the popup menu, select **Merge It**.

- The **Microsoft Word Mail Merge Wizard** dialogue box opens. Select the second option: **Create a new document and then link the data to it** and click **OK**.

- Word opens ready to create the standard letter. Press **Enter** about six times to leave some space at the top of the letter for a standard letterhead and to insert the date.

The following instructions use the **Mail Merge** task pane from Windows 2003. If you are using an earlier version of Word, you will have to insert the fields one-by-one using the **Insert Merge Fields** button on the **Mail Merge** toolbar.

- Word should have started with the Mail Merge task pane displayed (Figure 2.15).

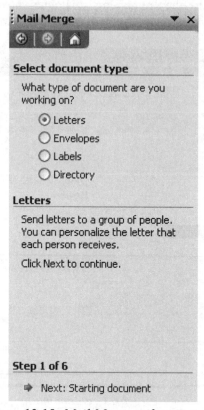

Figure 12.15: Mail Merge task pane

- Since we are creating a letter, leave **Letters** selected as the document type. Click **Next: Starting document**.

- Leave **Use the current document** selected, and click **Next: Select recipients**.

- Leave **Use an existing list** selected. Notice that Word knows about the query we had selected in Access when we started the mail merge—[**qryBusinessCustomer**]. Click **Next: Write your letter**.

- The next step is to add an address block, but first we need to give Word some hints about what our database fields actually mean. Press the **Match Fields** button on the **Database** toolbar.

- In the **Match Fields** dialogue box, set **First Name** to *Initials*, **Address 1** to *Street*, **City** to *Town*, **Address 2** to *Village* and **State** to *County*. Click **OK**.

- In the **Mail Merge** task bar, click **Address Block...**, and select the default format.

- Use **Greeting line...** to add *<<GreetingLine>>* a couple of lines below *<<AddressBlock>>*. Your letter should appear something like Figure 12.16.

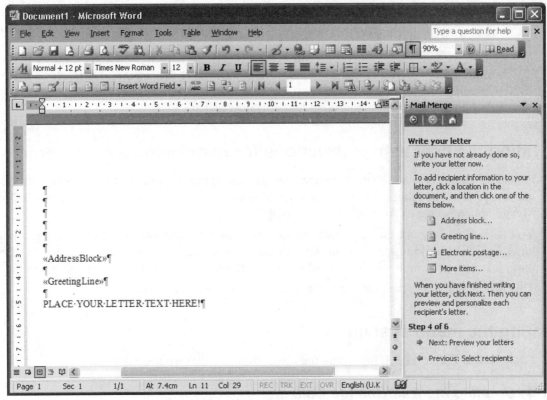

Figure 12.16: Design of the mail merge letter for business customers

- Click **Next: Preview your letters**. If the fields have been matched correctly, your letter should look like Figure 12.17.

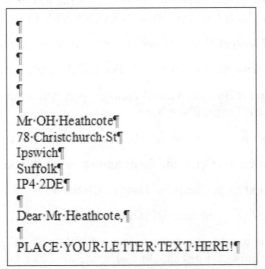

Figure 12.17: Preview of the mail merge letter for business customers

- Select Next: Complete the merge.

- Click Edit individual letters... to generate a letter for each selected customer, which can be printed (no need to do that now).

- Close without saving – you do not need to keep the letters, which are distinct from the master letter where the merge fields were placed. Save this master document as *Business Customers Letter* or some other suitable title, in a convenient directory. (It may be a good idea to save the letter in the same folder as the database.)

Providing the user with instructions for performing a mail merge

Instead of completely automating the mail merge, one option is simply to have clear instructions on how to print the letters, either in the User Manual, or displayed on the screen when the **Mail Merge** option is chosen from the menu, or both.

You should first try out the steps that the user will have to perform to use an existing standard letter, and then write instructions on how to do it. You can then create a new form to display these instructions, which will be opened when the user selects **Mail Merge** from your menu.

This is not included in the prototype, but you could do it as an exercise.

Creating the menu system

Look back at Figure 11.2. This shows the menu structure that we need to create.

Step 1: Creating the Add/Change Data menu

- In the database window, click the **Forms** tab and double-click **Create form in Design view**.

- A new blank form will appear. Click the **Label** tool and click and drag the cursor on the form where you want a heading to appear. Type the heading *Add/Change Data Menu*, and adjust the font style, size and position to match Figure 12.19.

- Make sure the **Control Wizards** tool is selected on the toolbar.

- Click the **Command Button** icon, and click and drag the cursor on the form as before.

- The first **Command Button Wizard** dialogue box will automatically appear. Select **Form Operations, Open Form**. Click **Next**.

- Specify **frmCustomer** as the form to be opened. Click **Next**.

- Select the option button **Open the form and show all the records** and click **Next**.

- Set the button **Text** to be *Customer Details*. Click **Next**.

- Name the button *OpenfrmCustomer*. Click **Finish**.

- Place another button on the form to open the Job Sheet, in the same way as already described. Your finished form should look something like Figure 12.19.

- Click on the small square at the top left hand corner, at the intersection of the ruler lines, using the RIGHT mouse button to display a popup menu. Select **Properties**.

- In the properties box, change the settings for **Scroll Bars**, **Record Selectors**, **Navigation Buttons** and border style as shown in Figure 12.18.

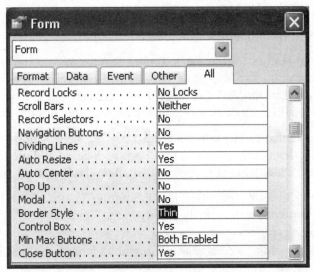

Figure 12.18: Setting the form properties

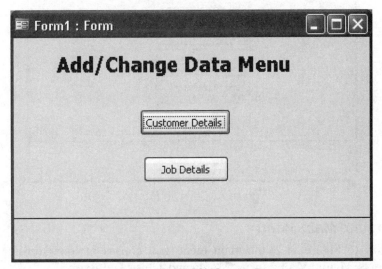

Figure 12.19: The Add/Change Data menu

- Note that a **Quit to Main Menu** option will have to be added later. Save the form as *fmnuAdd/ChangeData*.

Step 2: Creating the Reports menu

The Business Customers report is the only one to have been implemented so far, so although buttons may be placed for the other reports they will not have any actions attached to them.

- Create a new form in **Design View**, as before

- Place a heading on the form.

- Place a command button. Select Report Operations, Preview Report. Specify rptBusinessCustomer.

- Continue through the other dialogue boxes, giving your button the title *Business Customers*. Change properties as before.

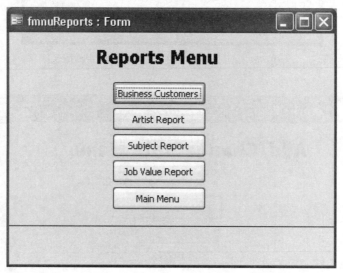

- Add command buttons for the *Artist Report*, *Subject Report*, *Job Value Report* and *Return to Main Menu* options. Since these buttons will not yet be operational, before you place the button you can turn off the wizard by deselecting the Control Wizards tool in the Design View toolbar. Then simply type the button titles straight onto the buttons.

- You can ensure that all the buttons are exactly the same size by selecting them (drag the cursor around them) and then selecting Format, Size, to Widest. Then repeat, selecting to Tallest. You can align them by selecting Align on the Format menu.

- The menu should look something like the one in Figure 12.20, but only the first button (Business Customers) will actually do anything. Test it now.

Figure 12.20: The Reports Menu

Step 3: Creating the Main Menu

Referring back to Figure 11.2, the main menu will consist of four items: **Add/Change Data Menu**, **Reports Menu**, **Mail Merge Menu** and **Close Database**. The first two of these have already been created. The **Main Menu** will be created in exactly the same way, by placing command buttons which open up the relevant submenus or close the database.

Finishing off the prototype

This step is left to you! You can complete the menu system, improve the appearance of the input screens, and add the other queries and reports. Or you can leave it just as it is, because this is sufficient to demonstrate exactly what the finished system will do.

Chapter 13 – Developing the Prototype

Objectives

By the end of this chapter you will have learned how to:

create and customise a combo box with and without using a wizard;

write a macro to find a particular record;

attach a macro to the event property of a control;

create Visual Basic modules using a variety of commands;

use variables in Visual Basic modules;

use the on-line help to get more information on command syntax.

Using the prototype as a design tool

Now that the prototype is finished, you can take a good look at it and perhaps even show it to the end-users to get their views. Look back at the original objectives and ask yourself in what ways the current system can be improved. Here are some suggestions for the A.B. Frames project:

- A combo box could be added to the **frmCustomer** form to look up any customer.

- The customer number could be automatically incremented. This could be achieved by using an **AutoNumber** field for the **CustomerID**, or using a Visual Basic module. This second option is more flexible because the user can specify a particular ID.

- Extra touches could be added to the **frmCustomer** form to make data entry easier and quicker; for example, the cursor could skip over the **Business Name** field unless the **Business Customer** field was ticked. The customer's initials and post code could be automatically converted to uppercase. Since most customers come from Ipswich, then as soon as *Ipswich* is entered, the county could be set equal to *Suffolk*.

- A button could be added to the **frmCustomer** form so that when a new customer is added, or an existing customer is looked up, the **frmJobSheet** form will automatically be opened with the customer ID, name and address displayed.

- In the **frmJobSheet** form, the **Job Total** and **Number of Items in Job** could be calculated automatically.

- In the **fsubItem** subform, a list box could be used for **Item Type** so that the user simply has to select a type rather than entering it each time. If a customer job includes an item of type **Restoration**, for example, the customer record could be automatically updated to tick the **Restoration** field.

♦ All the jobs for one customer could be displayed in a subform in the **frmCustomer** form. Then, when the user double-clicks a particular job number, the **frmJobSheet** form for that job could be automatically opened.

The next step in the project is to figure out how these ideas are to be implemented, and write up the Design Section of the final report. You can turn to the Design Section of the second project to see how this has been done.

The next three chapters of this book will show you how to implement all these ideas, many of which you may be able to modify for your own project. You will learn a lot from working through them, and once you are comfortable with writing Visual Basic modules and know what the possibilities are, you will find it very much easier to come up with a good design.

However, this book is not intended to be a complete Access and Visual Basic tutorial, so if you want to become a real expert you need to buy a good book—there are dozens available—which teaches your particular version of Access.

Creating a combo box to find records

Step 1: Using a wizard to create the combo box

One of the most common tasks in any database application is looking up an existing record. Adding a combo box to do this will be much easier for the user than using the standard 'Find' command. To create the combo box:

- Open the **frmCustomer** form in **Design** view.

- Make sure the **Control Wizards** tool is selected and then click the **Combo Box** tool.

- Click the **Combo Box** tool.

- Click the top of the form to the right of the title **Customer Details Form**. (You may need to move the heading over and enlarge the form.) The **Combo Box Wizard** starts, asking how you want to get the values it will display in the list.

- Select the third option, **Find a record on my form based on the value I selected in my combo box**, and then click **Next**.

- The wizard asks you which fields you want to include in the combo box. Double-click the **Surname** field to add it to the **Selected Fields** list, and then click **Next**.

- Drag the right side of the field selector in the **Surname** column to make it a bit narrower, and then click **Next**.

- The wizard asks what label you want for your combo box. Type *&Find Customer* and then click **Finish**.

Tip:
*Typing an ampersand character before the F (&Find Customer) turns **F** into a 'hot key', so that the user can activate the button either by pressing it or by pressing **Alt-F**.)*

Step 2: Trying out the combo box

- Click the **Form View** button on the toolbar.

- Click the arrow of the **Find Customer** combo box. A list of names will be displayed.

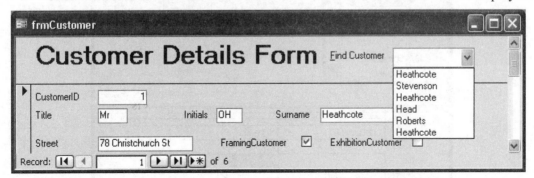

Figure 13.1: Combo box showing customer surnames

Step 3: Modifying the combo box

The combo box could be improved by displaying the names in alphabetical order, and displaying any particular surname only once, even if there is more than one customer named, say, Heathcote. (Later on we'll add other buttons to go to the Next or Previous record for a customer with the same surname as the one displayed.)

- Click the **Design View** button on the toolbar.

- Right-click the **Find Customer** combo box and then click **Properties** on the shortcut menu. The property sheet for the combo box will be displayed.

- Click the **All** tab in the property sheet to display all properties.

- Change the name of the combo box from **Combo41** or whatever it is now, to *FindIt*. (This will make it easier to refer to later on.)

- Click the **Row Source** property, and then click the **Build** button (...) on the right of the property box as in Figure 13.2.

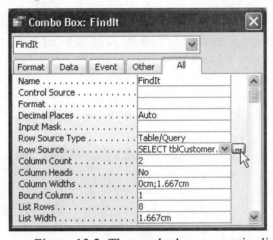

Figure 13.2: The combo box properties list

The Query Builder is displayed, and can be modified in any way you like.

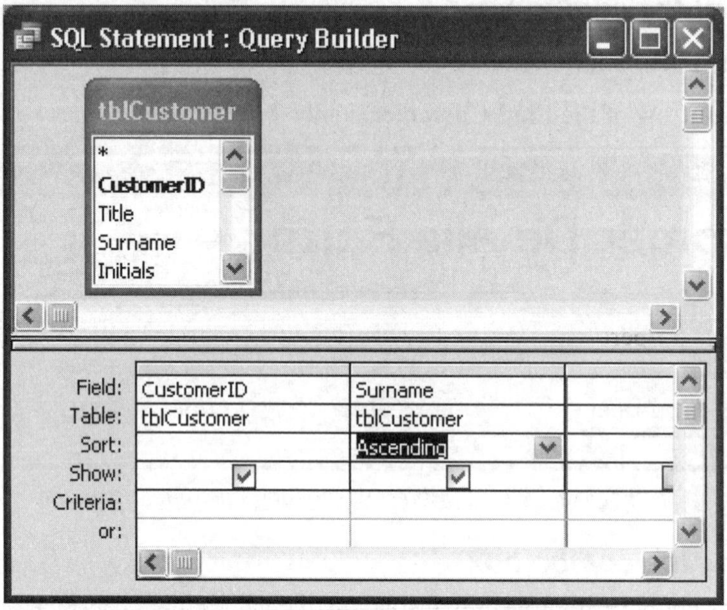

Figure 13.3: The Query Builder window for the combo box

- Click the **Sort** box underneath **Surname**, click the dropdown arrow, and then click **Ascending**.

- Close the **Query Builder** window, clicking **Yes** when asked if you want to save the changes to the query and SQL statement.

- For test purposes, you should make sure you have at least two customer records for different customers with the same surname, so, if necessary, switch to **Form View** and add more customers.

- Try out the combo box. The names should be in alphabetical order, but duplicates still show up in the list.

This is far as you can go without getting into programming! The wizard has set properties and added a Visual Basic event procedure behind the scenes; what you need to do now is create your own slightly different event procedure or macro. So far, the record does not change when you click in the list.

Programming with macros

Access offers two ways to write programs: with macros and with Visual Basic. A macro consists of one or more actions, and may contain conditions that enable you to build macros containing branches and loops just like a program. Macros are generally invoked by an *event* such as opening or closing a form, clicking a button or entering or leaving a particular field.

Step 1: Placing an Unbound control

- You've already done this when you created the **Find Customer** combo box.

The Row Source property now has to be defined, to tell Access where to get the values to display in the Combo Box. This can be done in one of two ways; by writing the SQL code directly into the Row Source property, or by letting Access generate the SQL from a Query. We'll do the latter.

Step 2: Defining the SQL for the Row Source

- In the properties sheet for the combo box, click **Row Source**.
- Click the **Build** button. If the **Show Table** dialogue box appears. Select **tblCustomer**, press **Add** and then **Close**.
- In the **Query Builder**, select the **CustomerID** column and press **Delete**.
- Edit the **Surname** field so that the **Criteria** row reads *Is Not Null*. (If a customer record has no surname entered, you don't want a blank line appearing in the combo box.)
- In the properties list, set **Column Count** to *1*, and delete the text of **Column Widths**. You need to do this because you have deleted the **CustomerID** column form the **Row Source**.
- Close the query and answer **Yes** when prompted to save.
- Check the SQL code that has been automatically generated. With the cursor somewhere in the **Row Source** property, press the **Zoom** key (**Shift-F2**) and the SQL will be displayed.
- Click **OK** and then change to **Form View** to try the combo box. It will still show duplicate surnames (make sure you have some in your test data) and, of course, selecting a particular surname won't have any effect because we have not yet added the appropriate event property.
- Go back to **Design View** and display the combo box property sheet again. Zoom in on the SQL in the Row Source, and edit it by adding in the word *DISTINCT* after SELECT (*SELECT DISTINCT [tblCustomer]...*), as shown in Figure 13.4.

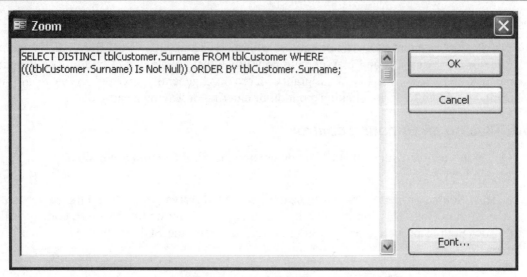

Figure 13.4: Automatically generated SQL code (after modification)

This will ensure that only one occurrence of each surname is displayed. Test your change.

Step 3: Creating a macro to find a record

- Click the **Design View** icon again and display the properties sheet for the combo box.

- In the **After Update** property, delete any text it contains and then click the **Build** button (3 dots) and the **Choose Builder** window will open. Select **Macro Builder** and press **OK**.

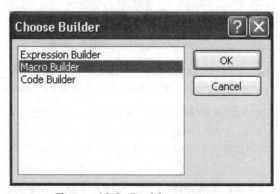

Figure 13.5: Building a macro

- In the next dialogue box, name the macro *mfrmCustomerFind* and press **OK**.

- The **Macro Builder** window will open.

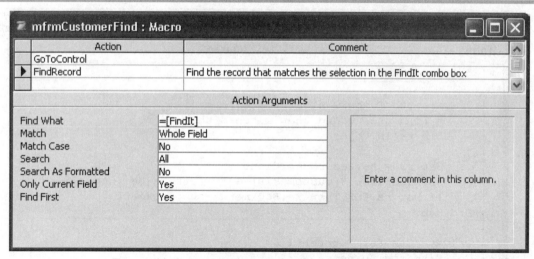

Figure 13.6: Writing a macro to find a customer record

- In the **Action** column, click the arrow and select **GoToControl**. In the **Control Name** (in the **Action Arguments** area in the lower half of the screen), enter *Surname*.

- On the next line in the **Action** column, click the arrow and select **FindRecord**. In the **Action Argument** named **Find What** enter *=[FindIt]*. This tells the macro to find the first record having the surname specified in the **FindIt** combo box.

- Add a comment to remind yourself what the macro does.

- Close the macro, answering **Yes** when asked if you want to save changes.

- Change to **Form View** and test the combo box.

Step 4: Add code to keep the combo box synchronised

You'll notice that when you go to a record by some means other than the combo box— for example, by using a navigation button to go to the next record—the surname displayed in the combo box doesn't change, which could confuse the user. You can add a line of code to the form's module to fix this problem.

- Open the form in **Design View**, or go to **Design View** if it is already open.

- Click the form selection box at the upper left corner of the form window (at the intersection of the rulers).

- Click the right mouse button and open the property sheet for the form.

- Click the **Event** tab in the property sheet.

- Click the **On Current** property, and then click the **Build** button (**...**).

- Select **Code Builder**, and then click **OK**.

- The form module for the **frmCustomer** form opens and displays the **Form_Current** event procedure.

- Add a line of code to the procedure:
  ```
  FindIt = Surname
  ```

```
ABFrames - Form_frmCustomer (Code)                    [_][□][X]

Form                        ▼   Current                        ▼

    Option Compare Database

    Private Sub Combo39_AfterUpdate()
        ' Find the record that matches the control.
        Dim rs As Object

        Set rs = Me.Recordset.Clone
        rs.FindFirst "[CustomerID] = " & Str(Nz(Me![Combo39], 0))
        If Not rs.EOF Then Me.Bookmark = rs.Bookmark
    End Sub

    Private Sub Form_Current()
        FindIt = Surname
    End Sub
```

Figure 13.7: Form module

This code sets the value of the combo box (which you named **FindIt** earlier on) to the
value of the **Surname** control in the current record.

- Close the module window, return to the **Form View** and test the combo box. Perfect, or a
  complete disaster?

Programming in Visual Basic

Visual Basic code is stored in *modules*. Each form and report in a database has its own attached
form module or *report module* for storing Visual Basic code – for example, the code attached to
each control in a form is stored in the form module. (A *control* is anything in a form, such as a
label, data field, combo box or control button.)

Most Visual Basic code that you write will belong to an individual form or report; however, if
you write code that applies to more than one form or report, you can store it in one or more
standard modules, which are separate objects in the database window.

Visual Basic code is held in *procedures*, each performing a single task. A module may contain
many procedures, one for each event you want to respond to, or task you want to perform. For
example, a Form module may have an **Open** procedure, a **Current** procedure, an **AfterUpdate**
procedure and so on. A command button on the form may have an **On Click** procedure and an
On DblClick procedure.

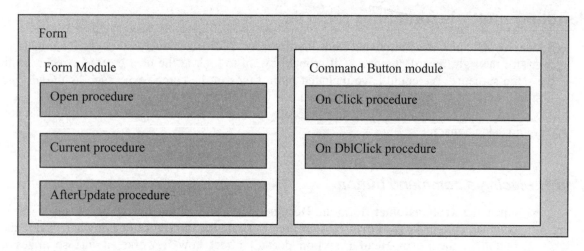

Figure 13.8: The relationship between forms, modules and procedures. Modules can also belong to reports, or be stored in a standard module in the database window.

You can use Visual Basic to perform almost any task that can be performed with macro actions. This is accomplished in two ways:

1. Equivalent statements, which duplicate the functions of certain macros. For example, the statement used in Figure 13.7

   ```
   FindIt = Surname
   ```

   is an example of an assignment statement. This could also have been written as

   ```
   Let FindIt = Surname
   ```

   The equivalent macro is the **SetValue** macro.

2. Using *methods.* Each object such as a form or control has its own set of methods. For example, to set the focus in the object **Surname**, you can use the **SetFocus** method, and write

   ```
   Surname.SetFocus
   ```

DoCmd is a rather special object in Visual Basic for Applications, with its own set of methods. In Visual Basic, the equivalent of the **FindIt** macro action (to find the first record containing "Smith" in the current field) is the instruction

```
DoCmd.FindRecord "Smith",,True,,True
```

This action has seven arguments (see Figure 13.6) and setting the third argument to *True* means that the search is case-sensitive; i.e. it does not find "SMITH" or "smith".

Notice that you can leave any of the arguments with their default values by omitting them, but you must remember to type a comma for each one you leave out.

Handling multiple matching records

So far, we have placed a button that finds the first record for a customer with a given surname. If this isn't the right record, the user will probably want to look at the next customer record with the same surname. We could have included more fields in the combo box, such as initials and first line of address. Instead we will place a **Next** button on the form, but this time we'll use a procedure instead of a macro. Procedures are very powerful, and allow you to do things that you can't do using a macro.

Step 1: Placing a command button

- Open the **frmCustomer** form in **Design View**, and if necessary, make space for a command button in the **Form Header** area by dragging the **Detail** line down. (Placing the button in the **Form Header** section doesn't affect how it works, it just separates it logically from the data entry area.)

- Make sure the **Control Wizards** tool is deselected, and then click the **Command Button** icon. Click in the header section where you want to place it. (Press **Cancel** if the **Command Button Wizard** dialogue box is displayed.)

- Type the caption *Next* on the button.

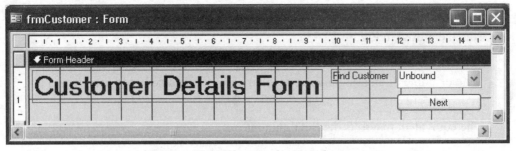

Figure 13.9: Placing the Next button

- Click the button using the right hand mouse button, and open the **Properties** box. In the **Name** property, type *Find Next*. (Note that you can have a space in a name, but when referring to it in a procedure, you must enclose it in square brackets.)

Step 2: Attaching code to locate the correct record

- Click the **On Click** event property and click the **Build** button (**...**).

- Select **Code Builder** from the **Choose Builder** dialogue box.

- Type the commands as shown below. Other macros associated with the form will also appear in the window (depending on your version of Access), but for now we're only interested in the **Find_Next_Click()** part. Note that the last argument (**Find First**) should be set to *False* because if it were left as *True*, the search would stop at the current record instead of finding the next record.

- Note that you can ignore case (i.e. uppercase, lowercase) when typing in Basic statements. Access checks the case and alters it if necessary when you move to the next line.

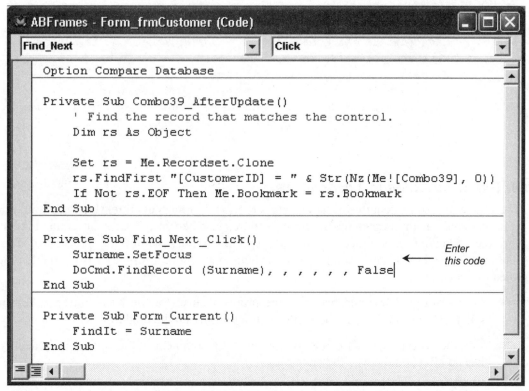

Figure 13.10: Code for the Next button

- Compile the code by selecting **Compile** on the **Debug** menu at the top of the screen. This will tell you if you have any syntax errors: if there are no errors, nothing appears to happen.

- Close the module window, return to **Form View** and try out your button.

It works fine, except that when it reaches the last matching record, it might be better if it displayed a message telling the user there were no more matching records. There are various options here: a message box could be displayed, or the caption on the button could be changed to say *No more matches*, or simply *No More*. We'll try that option.

Step 3: Planning your procedure

As your procedures get longer, you will need to plan them out and write down the steps in ordinary English or pseudocode before you try to code them.

If you have tried out your **Next** button, you'll notice that when the last matching record is reached, another click has no effect; the same record remains on screen. Therefore, we can test for the last matching record by checking whether the **CustomerID** remains unchanged when the **Next** button is pressed. If it does, then the caption will be changed. We need to save the current **CustomerID** in a variable, so that it can be compared with the **CustomerID** in the record that becomes current when **Next** is pressed.

Here is the pseudocode for the procedure which will be executed when the **Next** button is clicked:

```
Procedure Find Next
    Save the current CustomerID in a variable called CR
    Move the cursor to the Surname field
    Find the next record with the same surname
    (If there isn't one, the same record will remain current)
    If CustomerID = CR then    (the same record is still on screen)
        change the caption on the button to "No more"
    End If
End Proc
```

Step 4: Using variables in a procedure

The above procedure requires a variable to store the current **CustomerID**. You should declare your variables at the beginning of the procedure, just like in a Pascal program. Like Pascal, variables declared in a procedure are *local*, known only within the procedure. The **Dim** statement is used to declare variables; use the help to get more information on variable types and rules for names.

- Go to **Design View** and bring up the property sheet for the **Next** button. Click the **On Click** event property, and the **Build** button to bring up the module.

- Edit the procedure as shown below. Note that a comment in the code is preceded by ' and has no effect on the way the code runs.

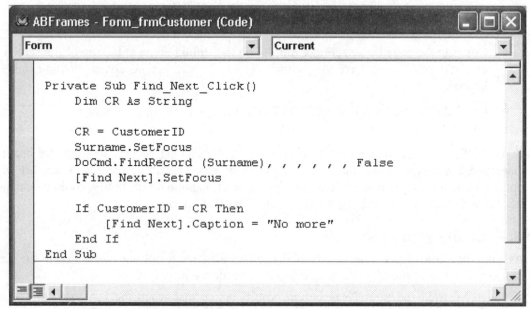

*Figure 13.11: The modified code for the **Next** button's **On Click** event*

- Compile the code to check for syntax errors.

- Save and test the modified code.

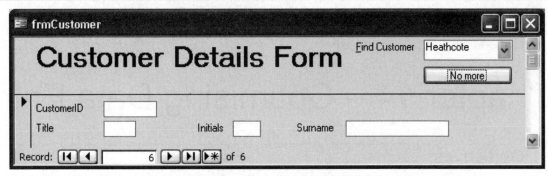

Figure 13.12: Changing the caption on the Next button

It works fine, apart from that, once the caption changes to **No more**, it doesn't change back to **Next** unless you close the form and reopen it. It needs to change back as soon as the user clicks any other control. To do this, we can attach some code to the button's **On Lost Focus** event.

- In the property sheet for the **Next** button, click in the **On Lost Focus** property, and click the **Build** button. Select **Code Builder** in the next dialogue box and add the following line of code:

```
[Find Next].Caption = "Next"
```

- Compile and test your code. It should work perfectly!

Using the help in Access 2000

The help is an invaluable aid to the programmer. For example to find out what the syntax and arguments of the **FindRecord** method are, use the help facility as follows:

- From the main menu select **Help**.

- Select **Microsoft Office Access Help**, and the **Access Help** task pane should appear. Type *FindRecord* in the **Search for** box and press **Enter**.

- Click **Actions**

- Click **FindRecord Action**

The Help screen will be displayed.

Chapter 14 – Optimising Data Entry

Objectives

By the end of this chapter you will have learned how to:

automatically increment the CustomerID number when adding a new record;

customise the tab order;

set the focus depending on the value(s) entered in another control;

automatically convert an entry to uppercase;

set default field values;

display values from one form in another form;

create customised error messages;

perform a calculation and display the results in a field of a form.

Providing data entry shortcuts

Data entry can be a tedious, time-consuming business, and anything you can do to make it easier will result in a more useful system for the end-user. The aim is to reduce the number of keystrokes and mouse-clicks required, by anticipating the data entry wherever possible and giving the user helpful messages immediately if they make an invalid entry.

Automatically incrementing the CustomerID

One way of automatically incrementing a key field such as **CustomerID** is to make its field type **AutoNumber**. Access then automatically assigns the next integer value whenever a new record is opened. However, this is often unsatisfactory because the number cannot be altered, so if the user wants some control over what numbers are allocated another method has to be used.

As with all programming, you need to think out the steps involved and write them down in ordinary English or pseudocode before you start entering code. Here is a pseudocode version:

```
Procedure AddCustomer
   Go to the last record
   Set CustID = value of CustomerID in this record
   If CustID = 0   Then            (i.e. this is the very first record)
      CustomerID = 1               (default to 1)
   Else
      Go to next record            (to bring up a new record)
      CustomerID = CustID + 1
   End If
   Move the cursor to the Title field  (save user an extra keystroke)
End Proc
```

Step 1: Using the wizard to place an Add Customer command button

We can get off to a flying start by using a wizard to automatically create some of the **On Click** event code for the **Add Customer** button. Looking at the pseudocode, the first thing that the code needs to do is to go to the last record.

- Open the frmCustomer form in Design View.

- Make sure the Control Wizards tool is selected.

- Click the Command Button icon and then click in the form header, next to the combo box.

- In the Command Button wizard dialogue box, select Record Navigation, and Go to Last Record. Click Next.

- Enter *Add Customer* in the Text box. Click Next.

- Name the button *AddCustomer*. Click Finish.

Figure 14.1: Placing the Add Customer command button

Step 2: Customising the code

- In **Design View**, open the **Properties** sheet for the **AddCustomer** button. Click in the **On Click** event property, and click the **Build** button (...).

- The code that has been automatically generated will be shown (see Figure 14.2). It includes an error procedure, to trap any errors and display a message if anything unexpected occurs. This part of the code can all be left as it stands.

```
Private Sub AddCustomer_Click()
On Error GoTo Err_AddCustomer_Click


    DoCmd.GoToRecord , , acLast

Exit_AddCustomer_Click:
    Exit Sub

Err_AddCustomer_Click:
    MsgBox Err.Description
    Resume Exit_AddCustomer_Click

End Sub
```

Figure 14.2: Code generated by the wizard

- Make changes to the code, following your pseudocode. Remember to declare the variable **CustID** using a **Dim** statement, and to add comments to explain what's happening. The additional code is shown below in Figure 14.3.

- Compile the code to check for syntax errors (**Debug**, **Compile**).

- Switch to **Form View** and test your code.

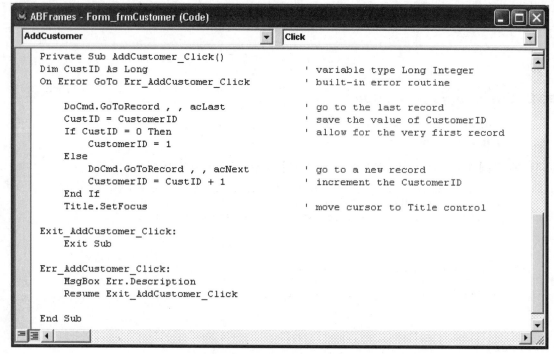

```
ABFrames - Form_frmCustomer (Code)

AddCustomer                            Click

Private Sub AddCustomer_Click()
Dim CustID As Long                     ' variable type Long Integer
On Error GoTo Err_AddCustomer_Click    ' built-in error routine

    DoCmd.GoToRecord , , acLast         ' go to the last record
    CustID = CustomerID                 ' save the value of CustomerID
    If CustID = 0 Then                  ' allow for the very first record
        CustomerID = 1
    Else
        DoCmd.GoToRecord , , acNext     ' go to a new record
        CustomerID = CustID + 1         ' increment the CustomerID
    End If
    Title.SetFocus                      ' move cursor to Title control

Exit_AddCustomer_Click:
    Exit Sub

Err_AddCustomer_Click:
    MsgBox Err.Description
    Resume Exit_AddCustomer_Click

End Sub
```

Figure 14.3: The finished code

Customising the form's tab order

In **Form View**, press **Add Customer** and tab through your form. Unless you have reset the tab order, the cursor jumps all over the place. Two improvements can be made:

♦ the tab order can be set so that the cursor goes through the form in a logical order; and

♦ the **Business Name** control can be skipped if **Business Customer** is not checked.

Step 1: Resetting the tab order

● Switch to **Design View**, and from the menu select **View, Tab Order**.

● In the dialogue box, select **Detail**.

Figure 14.4: Altering the tab order

● Look at the form to see which tab order would be most convenient for the user, and select and drag rows in the **Custom Order** list. Click **OK** when done.

● Test the form.

Step 2: Skipping the Business Name control if not relevant

To do this you need to write some code for the **BusinessCustomer** control's **Exit** property.

● Open the property sheet for the **BusinessCustomer** control (the tick box).

● Click in the **On Exit** event property and click the **Build** button (**...**).

● Select **Code Builder** and press **OK**.

● The code window opens. Enter the code shown in bold:

```
Private Sub BusinessCustomer_Exit(Cancel As Integer)
    'Skip the Business Name control if not a business customer
    If BusinessCustomer = True Then
        BusinessName.SetFocus
    Else
        CustomerNotes.SetFocus
    End If
End Sub
```

- Compile your code to check the syntax (choose Debug, Compile from the menu). If nothing happens, then you have no syntax errors – though there may be logic errors which will come to light when you try to run the code.

For example, suppose you have accidentally omitted the **End If**. When you compile the code, you'll get the following error message:

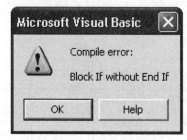

Figure 14.5: A compiler error message

- Close the code window when the code is free of syntax errors, return to **Form View** and try adding a new customer to test the **BusinessCustomer** control.

Setting default values in controls

You can speed up data entry by setting default values in controls wherever possible. In the **frmCustomer** form, we'll do two things to make data entry a little more convenient:

- Change **Initials** and **Postcode** to uppercase, in case they were accidentally entered in lowercase

- Let the **Town** default to *Ipswich*, and the **County** to *Suffolk*.

Step 1: Changing letters to uppercase

- In **Design View**, open the property sheet for the **Initials** control. Click in the **On Exit** property, and click the **Build** button.

- Click **Code Builder**.

- You need one of Visual Basic's built-in functions here, to convert a string to uppercase. There are several hundred functions and, if you aren't sure if a function exists to do what you want, you can use the **Object Browser** to look through them. Click the **Object Browser** icon now. (The icon may not be visible unless the code window is open.)

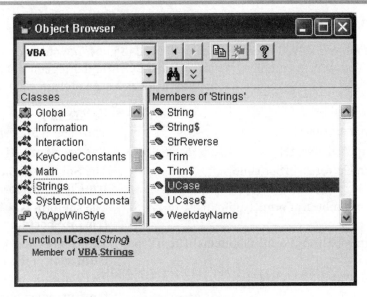

Figure 14.6: The Object Browser

- In the top left-hand box (*<<All Libraries>>*) select **VBA**.

- Since you are looking for a string function, click **Strings**.

- Scroll down the **Members of 'Strings'**, and select **UCase**, which is the function you want. In the bottom of the window, you can see its syntax (it takes a single String parameter).

- Back in the code window, type the following:

```
Private Sub Initials_Exit(Cancel As Integer)
   ' Change Initials to uppercase
   Initials = UCase(Initials)
End Sub
```

- Close the code window and, in a similar way, enter code in the **On Exit** event property for **PostCode**.

- Test your changes.

Step 2: Setting a default value in a control

- Open the property sheet for **Town**.

- We want to set the default value of **Town** to *Ipswich*. Which property should this code be attached to? **Before Update**, **After Update**, **On Entry**, **On Exit**? You have to be careful not to change an entry that the user has already made, back to **Ipswich**. In fact the property you need to attach the code to is a data property, not an event property.

- Find the **Default Value** data property, click in it and type = *"Ipswich"*.

- Similarly, set the default value for the county to *Suffolk*, if you did not already do so when building the prototype.

- Save and test your changes.

Referring to database objects

As you get more involved in coding, you will need to know how to refer to controls in forms and subforms. You write a complete identifier name by stringing together objects that contain other objects. Access uses an exclamation mark or a dot as a separator for each name. For example:

Identifier	**Refers to**
Forms![frmCustomer]	The open **frmCustomer** form
Reports![rptArtistName]	The open **rptArtistName** report
Forms![frmCustomer]![Surname]	The **Surname** control on the open **frmCustomer** form
Forms![frmJobSheet].Form![fsubItems]	The subform **fsubItems** of the **frmJobSheet** form
Forms![frmJobSheet].Form![fsubItems]![ItemType]	The **ItemType** control on the subform **fsubItems** of the **frmJobSheet** form
Forms![frmCustomer].[Caption]	The **Caption** property of the open **frmCustomer** form
Forms![frmCustomer]![Surname].[ForeColor]	The **ForeColor** property of the **Surname** control in the open **frmCustomer** form
Me![Surname]	The **Surname** control on the current open form

Notes:

♦ a dot is used as the separator when the next word is an Access-defined keyword like **Form**, **Caption** or **ForeColor**.

♦ an exclamation mark is used as the separator when the next word is user-defined, such as **[frmCustomer]**.

♦ you don't, strictly speaking, need the square brackets round an identifier when the identifier is a single word like **Surname**, but you must use the brackets when the object name is more than one word, like **[frmCustomer Details]**.

♦ a form is referred to using the name **Forms**, whereas a subform is referred to using the object name **Form** – a poor choice of keyword but we're stuck with it.

♦ a form must be open when code containing any reference to it is run.

♦ the keyword **Me** can be used to refer to the currently active form.

♦ you can get further information from the help by looking up *Naming Objects*.

Entering details of a new job

When a customer comes into the shop to buy a picture, or to have a picture restored or framed, a job sheet is filled in manually. These job sheets are going to be entered into the computer at a later time – perhaps at the end of the day or week (an example of *batch processing*). You therefore have to think what would be the easiest way for this to be done.

Try to imagine the different situations which will arise. The user might:

- want to enter a job for a new customer;
- want to enter a job for an existing customer;
- not know whether the customer details are already in the database.

There are many different ways of tackling this problem, using Visual Basic modules. You could, for example:

- open a new job sheet (**frmJobSheet**), and have a facility on the form to look up the customer surname, entering details automatically into the job sheet if the customer is already on file, or if not, asking the user if they want to enter customer details now. The customer form would then open for data entry and, when completed, control would return to the job sheet with the customer details filled in.

OR

- open the **frmCustomer** form so that the correct customer can be located, or details of a new customer entered, and have a command button which will open a new job sheet with all of the customer details filled in automatically.

The second approach has been selected in this project.

When a new job is to be entered:

```
Open the frmCustomer form
Look up the Customer surname using the combo box and, if needed, the
Next button.
If the customer's details are not already on file Then
  Click the Add Customer button and add the details
End If

Click the AddJob button (still to be created)
(Try and anticipate any errors the user might make)
If Customer name has not been entered Then
  Display message "Please enter customer information before entering job"
Else
  Open the frmJobSheet form, showing the relevant customer details.
End If
When the job sheet has been entered, click a 'Return to Customer
Details' button (still to be created).
```

Step 1: Placing the Add Job command button

- Open the **frmCustomer** form in **Design** view.

- Make sure the **Control Wizards** tool is selected.

- Click the **Command Button** tool.

- Click just under the **Add Customer** button in the form header.

- In the Command Button Wizard dialogue box, select Form Operations, Open Form. Click Next.

- Select frmJobSheet as the form you would like the command button to open. Click Next.

- Select the first option Open the form and find specific data to display. Click Next.

- Select CustomerID in both the frmCustomer form and the frmJobSheet form and click the < - > button in the middle (Figure 14.7). Click Next.

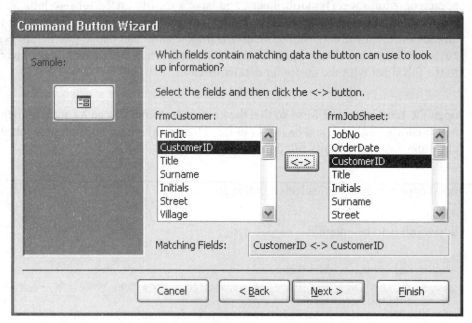

Figure 14.7: Linking Customer and Jobs

- Enter **Add Job** as the **Text** to display. Click **Next**.

- Enter **AddJob** as the name of the button. Click **Finish**.

- Adjust the size and font on the button if required.

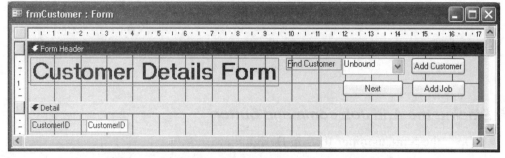

*Figure 14.8: The new **Add Job** command button*

We now have to add code to display the error message *Please enter customer information before entering job* if the user attempts to add a job from a blank **frmCustomer** form. This code has to be attached to the **On Click** property of the **Add Job** button.

Step 2: Customise the Add Job button

- Click the **Add Job** button with the right hand mouse button.

- Choose the **Build Event...** option from the popup menu. (This is an alternative way of opening the code window.) The code that was automatically created by the **Command Button Wizard** appears as shown in Figure 14.9.

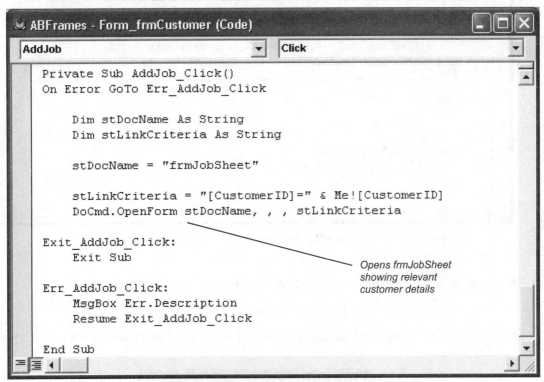

```
ABFrames - Form_frmCustomer (Code)

AddJob                              Click

Private Sub AddJob_Click()
On Error GoTo Err_AddJob_Click

    Dim stDocName As String
    Dim stLinkCriteria As String

    stDocName = "frmJobSheet"

    stLinkCriteria = "[CustomerID]=" & Me![CustomerID]
    DoCmd.OpenForm stDocName, , , stLinkCriteria
                                          Opens frmJobSheet
Exit_AddJob_Click:                        showing relevant
    Exit Sub                              customer details

Err_AddJob_Click:
    MsgBox Err.Description
    Resume Exit_AddJob_Click

End Sub
```

*Figure 14.9: Code attached to the **On Click** property of the **Add Job** button*

- Amend the lines of code under the second **Dim** statement:

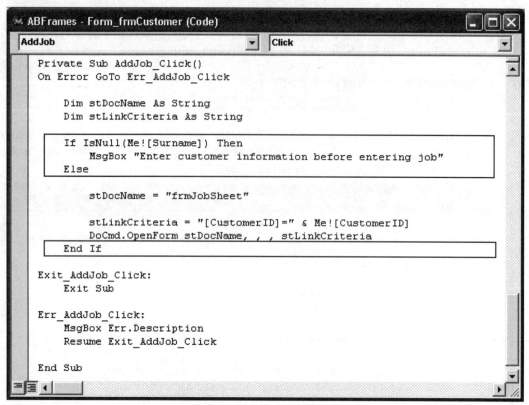

Figure 14.10: The amended code (the rest of the code stays as it is)

- Compile the code to make sure you have not made any syntax errors.

- Save the code, close the window and switch to **Form View**.

- Go to a new record and then press the **Add Job** button. The following message should be displayed:

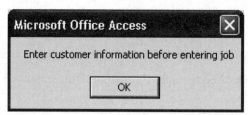

Figure 14.11: Displaying a customised error message

- Clear the message, go to a customer record and try again. If you try to return to a different record without filling in the **Surname** field, you may get an error message. This is because you have created a new record that is missing a compulsory field. To exit the record, type anything in the **Surname** field, then delete the whole record using **Edit**, **Delete Record** from the menu.

Customising the frmJobSheet form

When you display an existing customer's record on screen and press **Add Job**, **frmJobSheet** displays the first job for that customer. You can scroll through all the jobs for that customer until you open up a blank **Job Sheet**. If the customer has had no previous jobs, an empty form is displayed. Either way, the new blank **Job Sheet** does not display the customer name and address, which is what we want it to do. We have to add the code to do this.

Two questions need to be answered:

- ♦ what are the steps to be coded?

- ♦ what event(s) should the code be attached to?

We'll turn our attention next to the **Job Sheet** form. We can attach most of the required code to the **On Open** property of this form. The pseudocode for the procedure is as follows:

```
Procedure Form_Open
    If frmCustomer form is open Then
       Go to the last job record for this customer
       If JobNo is not empty Then        (customer already has at least
                                          one job record)
          Go to the next record
       End If
       Make the CustomerID field in this form equal to the
               CustomerID field in the frmCustomer form
    Else
       Display a message "The Customer Details form must be open"
    End If
End Proc
```

Writing your own functions

Before writing the procedure **Form_Open**, we need to write a general function that will test whether a form is open, returning the value *True* if it is, and *False* otherwise. The function will be stored in a global module named **Misc**.

Step 1: Writing a general function

- In the database window, click the **Modules** tab.

- Click the **New** button.

Microsoft creates a new standard module and displays it in the module window. From here, you can enter Visual Basic code and create general functions and procedures which can be called from anywhere.

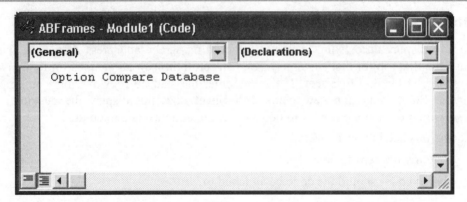

Figure 14.12: The module window

 • Click the **Insert Procedure** tool on the toolbar (in Access 2003 this may be in a submenu coming from the button for one of the other insert tools), or select **Insert**, **Procedure** from the menu.

• Microsoft Access displays the **Add Procedure** dialogue box, where you specify the name and type of the procedure you want to create.

• In the **Name** box, type *IsOpen*.

• In the **Type** box, select the **Function** option. Click **OK**.

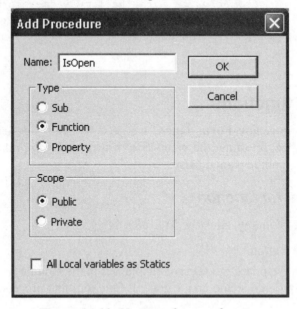

Figure 14.13: Naming the new function

Using SysCmd to test whether a form is open

Visual Basic and Access Basic include a useful function named **SysCmd** which can be used to return information about the state of a specified database object. It can be used to indicate whether the object (such as a form) is open, is a new object, or has been changed but not saved. The help gives a full explanation and examples of its use.

CurrentView is a form property which has the following settings:

0   if the form is displayed in **Design View**

1   if the form is displayed in **Form View**

2   if the form is displayed in **Datasheet View**.

Step 2: Test whether a form is open

- Type the following code:

```
Public Function IsOpen(ByVal StrFormName As String) As Boolean
' Returns True if the specified form is open in form view

    Const conDesignView = 0
    Const conObjStateClosed = 0
    IsOpen = False
    If SysCmd(acSysCmdGetObjectState, acForm, StrFormName) <> _
              conObjStateClosed Then
       If Forms(StrFormName).CurrentView <> conDesignView Then
          IsOpen = True
       End If
    End If
End Function
```

> *When continuing a line of code onto another line, put " _"*
> *(space, underscore) at the end of the line.*

(Note that you will have to replace the default function heading with the one shown above.)

- Click the **Compile** tool to check for syntax errors.

- Close the module, saving it as *basMisc*.

Step 3: Adding code to the On Open form property

- Open the **frmJobSheet** form in **Design View** and click the **Form** box (at the intersection of the ruler lines) with the right-hand mouse button.

- Open the properties window and click the **Build** button to the right of the **On Open** event property. Select **Code Builder** from the **Choose Builder** dialogue.

- Enter the code shown on the next page between the **Private Sub** and **End Sub** lines, each instruction on a single line:

```
Private Sub Form_Open(Cancel As Integer)
    If IsOpen("frmCustomer") Then
        DoCmd.GoToRecord , , acLast          ' go to last record
        If Not IsNull(Me![JobNo]) Then       ' if customer has a record
            DoCmd.GoToRecord , , acNext       ' open a new one
        End If
        Forms![frmJobSheet]![CustomerID]
    =Forms![frmCustomer]![CustomerID]
        JobNo.SetFocus
    Else                                      ' form is not open
    MsgBox "The Customer Details form must be open before you can enter a
        job"
        DoCmd.Close acForm, "frmJobSheet"
    End If
End Sub
```

- Compile the code to make sure you have not made any syntax errors.

- Save and close the code window, and test your code thoroughly.

*Note: Closing **frmJobSheet** without entering a job saves a record with a **JobNo** of 0, and the next occasion will cause an error message about creating duplicate values. Press **Esc** first to delete the record. The form must be closed for the **On Open** event to be triggered.*

Automatic calculations

The form still has several weaknesses, which your testing should bring to light. We'll address at least some of them. First of all, we'll look at how to automatically calculate and enter the job value and the number of items in the job. Two functions will help here: **DSum** and **DCount**. Look up the details of usage and syntax in the help.

It's a little difficult to decide which event to attach the code to, since we can't really anticipate what the user will do immediately after entering one or more items. One solution is to attach code to the **On Enter** event for both **JobValue** and **ItemsInJob**. The user will have to click in, or tab into, those fields for the calculations to be done.

Step 3: Automatic calculation of Job Value and Items in Job

- Open the **frmJobSheet** form in **Design** View, and open the property sheet for the **JobValue** control.

- Click the **On Enter** property, and click the **Build** button, then **Code Builder**.

- Type the following all on one line:

- Forms![frmJobSheet]![JobValue] = DSum("[ItemValue]", "tblItem",

- "[JobNo]=Forms![frmJobSheet]![JobNo]")

- Copy this line to the clipboard for use in a moment.

- Compile, save and close the code window.

- Click the **ItemsInJob** control.

- In the **On Enter** property, click the **Build** button, and again use **Code Builder**.

- Type the following all on one line (or paste and edit the line typed in above—the differences are in bold):

- Forms![frmJobSheet]![**ItemsInJob**] = **DCount**("[**ItemNo**]", "tblItem",

- "[JobNo]=Forms![frmJobSheet]![JobNo]")

- Compile, save and close the code window.

- Test your changes by opening the **frmJobSheet** from the **frmCustomer** form and entering a new job for an existing customer. Remember to click in **JobValue** and **ItemsInJob** after entering the item(s) to get them automatically calculated.

Step 4: Adding a form title, and a button to return to the Customer Details form

- Switch to Design View for frmJobSheet.

- Drag the Form Header down to make room for a form title and the new control button.

- Use the Label tool to add the form title *Job Details Form* to the form.

- Adjust the font and size to your liking.

- Click the Command Button tool.

- Click next to the heading to place the Command button.

- In the first wizard dialogue box, select Form Operations, Close Form. Click Next.

- Enter *Return to Customer Details* as the Text to display on the button. Click Next.

- Name the button *ReturnToCustomer*. Click Finish.

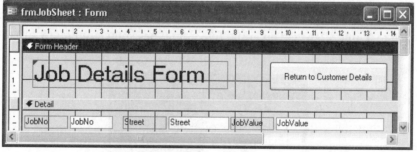

*Figure 14.14: Placing the **Return to Customer Details** button*

Smartening up the fsubItem Subform

The design of the second project specifies that, in the **fsubItem** subform, a list box will be used for **Item Type** so that the user just has to select from the list rather than typing in *Restoration*, *Framing*, etc. When the user tabs out of the **ItemType** field, the relevant field on the **tblCustomer** table will be automatically updated – for example, if **ItemType** is set to **Restoration**, the field **RestorationCustomer** on the **tblCustomer** table will be set to *True*. It will also be necessary to 'refresh' the open **frmCustomer** form to reflect any changes made in the **frmJobSheet** form, so that these are shown when the **frmJobSheet** form is closed.

Step 1: Creating a new table to hold item types

- In the Database window select Tables, New, Design View.

- The table needs only one field, ItemType. Leave it as a text field.

- Select the row and click the Primary Key icon to make this the primary key field.

- Set Allow Zero Length to *No*.

- Click the Save icon and name the table *tblItemType*.

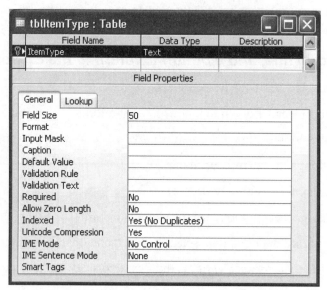

*Figure 14.15: The **tblItemType** table*

- Switch to **Table View** and enter the five item types shown in Figure 14.16.

Figure 14.16: Item Types

- Save and close the table.

Step 2: Make the ItemType control in the fsubItems subform a list box

- Open fSubItems in Design View.

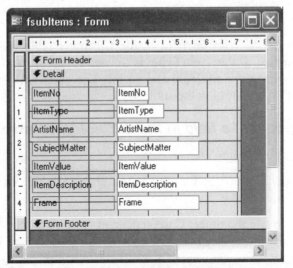

*Figure 14.17: The **fsubItems** subform*

- Click the **ItemType** field and press the **Delete** key to delete the field, which is to be replaced by a list box control.

- Make sure the **Control Wizards** tool is selected.

- Click the **List Box** tool, and then click in the space left by the deleted **ItemType**.

- On the first page, keep the first option **I want the list box to look up the values in a table or query**. Click **Next**.

- Select **tblItemType** as the table. Click **Next**.

- Click the arrow to move **ItemType** to the list of selected fields. Click **Next**.

- Select **ItemType** as a sort field, and click **Next**.

- Adjust the width in the next dialogue box if you like, or leave it as it is. Click **Next**.

- Select the second option **Store that value in this field**. Specify **ItemType** as the field to store it in. Click **Next**.

- Give the list box the label *Item Type* and click **Finish**.

- Click in the list box with the right mouse button and display its property sheet.

- Type *ItemType* in the **Name** property, and make sure that *ItemType* is in the **Control Source** property.

- Set the **Tab Index** property to *1*, so that it will get the focus after the **ItemNo** control. All the other tab index numbers will automatically adjust themselves.

- Save and close **fsubItems**.

- Test the changes by opening the **frmCustomer** form, selecting a suitable customer and adding a new job. You can alter the field widths in the subform while in **Form View** so that they are all visible.

The next step is to set the relevant field in the Customer table to *True* when the **ItemType** changes – for example, if the **ItemType** is *Framing*, the **FramingCustomer** field in the **tblCustomer** table will be set to *True*, and so on. The code will be attached to the **On Exit** property of the **ItemType** control in the subform.

Step 3: Automatic update of a field in the tblCustomer table

- Open fsubItems in Design View.

- Open the property sheet for ItemType, and click the On Exit property. Click the Build button (…), Code Builder.

- We are going to use the Select Case statement here. (You can look up details in the help under *Selection Statements*.) Enter the code as shown in Figure 14.18.

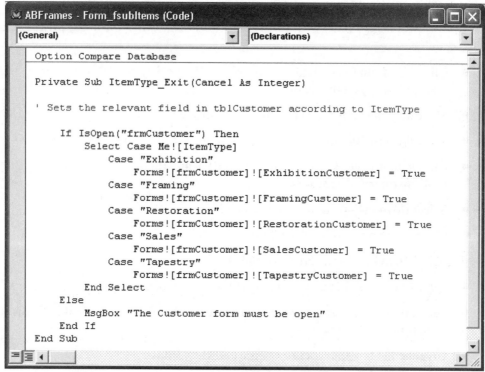

```
ABFrames - Form_fsubItems (Code)

(General)                              (Declarations)

Option Compare Database


Private Sub ItemType_Exit(Cancel As Integer)

' Sets the relevant field in tblCustomer according to ItemType

    If IsOpen("frmCustomer") Then
        Select Case Me![ItemType]
            Case "Exhibition"
                Forms![frmCustomer]![ExhibitionCustomer] = True
            Case "Framing"
                Forms![frmCustomer]![FramingCustomer] = True
            Case "Restoration"
                Forms![frmCustomer]![RestorationCustomer] = True
            Case "Sales"
                Forms![frmCustomer]![SalesCustomer] = True
            Case "Tapestry"
                Forms![frmCustomer]![TapestryCustomer] = True
        End Select
    Else
        MsgBox "The Customer form must be open"
    End If
End Sub
```

*Figure 14.18: Code for the **On Exit** property of **ItemType***

- Compile, save and exit. Test this new feature.

Chapter 15 – Helping the User to Look Up Information

Objectives

By the end of this chapter you will have learned how to:

write code to enable the user to look up all jobs for one customer;

use global variables;

test user actions and respond accordingly;

refresh a form so that it reflects changes made in another form.

Adding the facility to look up jobs

One of the user's requirements was to be able to quickly look up all the jobs for one customer. To do this, we can put a subform in the **frmCustomer** form showing **JobNo**, **ItemsInJob**, **Date**, **JobValue** and **Notes**. Then we can add code so that, when the user double-clicks a job number, the **frmJobSheet** form for that job is opened.

Step 1: Creating a Jobs subform

- Close all open forms and from the **Database** window select **Forms**, **New**.

- Select **Autoform:Datasheet** and **tblJob** and press **OK**.

- The wizard creates the form and displays it on screen in **Form View**. Close the form, and when asked if you want to save it, click **Yes** and name it *fsubJobs*.

- Open the **frmCustomer** form in **Design View**. You may need to drag the footer section down to make room for the new subform, which will be placed under the rest of the data.

- Rearrange the wondows so that you can see both the **Database** window (with the **fsubJobs** icon visible) and the **frmCustomer** form.

- Drag the **fsubJobs** icon onto the space you have made for the subform on the **frmCustomer** form.

- Delete the field and label for **CustomerID**, and adjust the position of the other fields.

- Switch to **Form View** and have a look at the form. You can adjust column widths to make the form look something like the one shown in Figure 15.1. If the settings for column widths change back to what they were when you close and open the form, then try opening **fsubJobs** in **Datasheet** view to adjust the column widths.

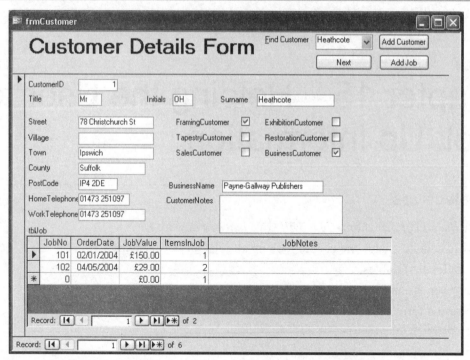

Figure 15.1: Placing the fsubJobs subform in the frmCustomer form

Using global variables

The idea is that when the user double-clicks the job number, the job sheet for that job will be displayed. However, we have already attached code to the **On Open** property of **frmJobSheet**, which is executed when the user clicks the **Add Job** button. We want different code to execute when **frmJobSheet** is opened by double-clicking the **JobNo** control in the subform. In this case, an existing job must be displayed, rather than a new job sheet.

We can get round this by setting a **Boolean** variable called **DisplayJob** to *True* when the user double-clicks **JobNo**. Then, in the code attached to the **On Open** property of the job sheet form, we can add an **If...Then...Else** statement so that one set of statements runs if the **Add Job** button click event caused the form to open, and another set of statements runs if the **On DblClick** event from **JobNo** opened the form.

Up to now, all the variables we have used have been declared within the procedures they were used in. These are called *procedure-level variables* and their *scope* is the procedure in which they are declared. In other words, they are not recognised outside the procedure.

There are three scoping levels:

Procedure-level scope: variables are declared in the procedure and not recognised outside it

Private module-level scope: variables declared in the **Declarations** section of a module as private

Public module-level scope: variables can be used throughout the database.

(For more detailed information, look up *Understanding Scope* in the help.)

Since we want to pass a variable's value from one module to another, it has to be declared in a database module as a Public variable.

Step 2: Declaring public (global) variables

- Open the database window and click the **Modules** tab. Select **basMisc**, and click **Design**.

- The code window opens. Enter the two lines of code shown in Figure 15.2 to declare two variables **DisplayJob** and **JobNum**.

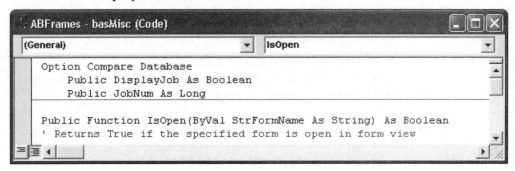

```
ABFrames - basMisc (Code)

(General)                                    IsOpen

    Option Compare Database
        Public DisplayJob As Boolean
        Public JobNum As Long


    Public Function IsOpen(ByVal StrFormName As String) As Boolean
    ' Returns True if the specified form is open in form view
```

*Figure 15.2: Declaring the global variables **DisplayJob** and **JobNum***

- Close and save the module.

Step 3: Adding code to the On DblClick event

- Open fsubJobs in Design View.

- Click JobNo with the right mouse button and open its property sheet.

- Click the On Dbl Click event property, open the code window, and enter the code shown in Figure 15.3.

- Close and save the code window and subform.

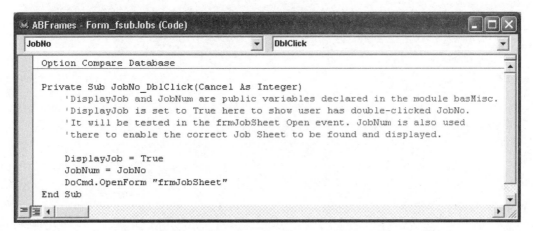

```
ABFrames - Form_fsubJobs (Code)

JobNo                                        DblClick

    Option Compare Database

    Private Sub JobNo_DblClick(Cancel As Integer)
        'DisplayJob and JobNum are public variables declared in the module basMisc.
        'DisplayJob is set to True here to show user has double-clicked JobNo.
        'It will be tested in the frmJobSheet Open event. JobNum is also used
        'there to enable the correct Job Sheet to be found and displayed.

        DisplayJob = True
        JobNum = JobNo
        DoCmd.OpenForm "frmJobSheet"
    End Sub
```

*Figure 15.3: The **On Dbl Click** event code*

Step 4: Modifying the frmJobSheet On Open event code

- Open **frmJobSheet** in **Design View** and display the code window for the **On Open** event property.

- Amend the existing code as shown below (new lines shown in bold):

```
Private Sub Form_Open(Cancel As Integer)
    If IsOpen("frmCustomer") Then

        ' DisplayJob is set in the frmCustomer form to:
        ' - TRUE when a user double-clicks JobNo in the fsubJobs
        ' - FALSE when the user clicks the AddJob button.

        If DisplayJob = False Then
            DoCmd.GoToRecord , , acLast
            If Not IsNull(Me![JobNo]) Then
                DoCmd.GoToRecord , , acNext
            End If
            Forms![frmJobSheet]![CustomerID] =
                    Forms![frmCustomer]![CustomerID]
        Else
            ' user wants to display a job whose number was stored in
            ' JobNum in the double-click event code in fsubJobs
            ' so look for that job and display it
            JobNo.SetFocus
            DoCmd.FindRecord jobNum
        End If
    Else
        MsgBox "The Customer Details form must be open before
                                    you can enter a job"
        DoCmd.Close acForm, "frmJobSheet"
    End If
End Sub
```

Step 5: Modify the Add Job code in the frmCustomer form

- Open the **frmCustomer** form in **Design View**. Click the **Add Job** button with the right mouse button and display the property sheet.

- Click the **On Click** event property, and click the **Build** button.

- Amend the existing code by adding in the three lines shown in bold below:

```
Private Sub AddJob_Click()
On Error GoTo Err_AddJob_Click

    Dim stDocName As String
    Dim stLinkCriteria As String

    If IsNull(Me![Surname]) Then
        MsgBox "Enter customer information before entering job"
    Else
        'DisplayJob is a global variable defined in basMisc
        'and tested in frmJobSheet On Open
        DisplayJob = False
        stDocName = "frmJobSheet"

        stLinkCriteria = "[CustomerID]=" & Me![CustomerID]
        DoCmd.OpenForm stDocName, , , stLinkCriteria
    End If

Exit_AddJob_Click:
    Exit Sub

Err_AddJob_Click:
    MsgBox Err.Description
    Resume Exit_AddJob_Click

    End Sub
```

- Compile and save the code, and close the code window

- Switch to **Form View** and test the **Add Job** button and the double-click of **JobNo** in the subform.

You may notice that when you add a new job, it is not shown in the subform when you return to the **frmCustomer** form. If you go to a different record, and then return to the original record, the new job will appear. We can add code to 'refresh' the current form so that the changes appear immediately in the current record.

The **Refresh** method tells Access to update the data displayed on the form with the current values from an underlying table.

Step 6: Refreshing the frmCustomer form when a new job is added

- Open the **frmJobSheet** in **Design View**. Click the **Return to Customer Details** button with the right mouse button and display the property sheet.

- Click the **On Click** property, and click the **Build** button to open up the code window.

- Add the three lines of code shown in Figure 15.4 just before the **DoCmd.Close** command:

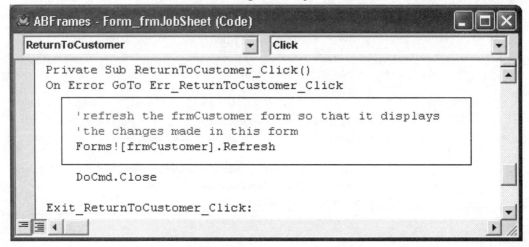

Figure 15.4: Refreshing the frmCustomer form

- Compile your code, save and return to the database window.

- Test the changes.

Putting finishing touches to data entry forms

When you test your input forms thoroughly, you will find that there are many finishing touches that you can add to make them even better: reorganising the layout of the forms, changing colours and fonts, inserting extra default values and validations, replacing Access messages with customised error messages, adding buttons to *Return to Main Menu*, and so on. Hopefully you now have enough knowledge and skills at your fingertips to be able to add all these touches to your own project.

Try adding an event procedure to the **JobNo** field on **frmJobSheet** to display an error message if the user leaves the ID as 0 and then moves out of the field.

Chapter 16 – Concentrating on Output

Objectives

By the end of this chapter you will have learned how to:

allow the user to specify a condition in a query;

perform the mail merge from Access;

make the main menu load automatically on start-up;

add a password.

Querying the database

In the last two chapters we have been concentrating on getting data *in* to the database. Now we turn our attention to how to get the required information *out* of the database in a suitable format; for example, for on-screen viewing, printing in a report or as letters to selected customers.

In the prototype, two queries were created and saved: **qryCustomerJob** was used for the **frmJobSheet** form, and **qryBusinessCustomer** formed the basis for the report of all business customers.

Several more queries have been created for the finished project; we'll go through the steps for creating the query designed to pick out of all of those customers who have had jobs totaling more than a certain value (specified by the user at run time). None of the other queries will use any new or different techniques.

Step 1: Creating the qryJobValue query

- From the **Database** window, click the **Queries** tab and select **New**. Use the **Design View**.

- In the **Show Table** dialogue box, add **tblCustomer** and **tblJob**. **Close** the dialogue box.

- Place the following fields in the table shown at the bottom of the screen by double-clicking them or dragging them:

- **Title, Initials, Surname, Street, Village, Town, County, Postcode (from tblCustomer) CustomerID, JobValue (from tblJob)**

- Click the **Totals** tool in the toolbar. This will make an extra **Total** row visible in the table.

- In the **JobValue** column, click the **Total** cell and select **Sum**. This will automatically calculate the sum of all jobs for each customer.

- In the **Criteria** row of the **JobValue** column, enter

  >=[Please enter minimum total job value]

  (The >= specifies that you are looking for customers whose job values are *greater than or equal to* the value entered when the query is executed.)

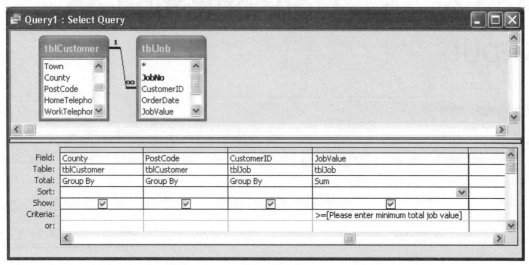

*Figure 16.1: Entering a **Sum** function and variable criteria*

- Test the query by pressing the **Run** tool.

- A dialogue box will appear, asking you to enter a minimum value. Enter a suitable value.

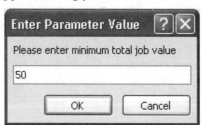

Figure 16.2: Allowing the user to specify a value

- Switch back to **Design View**. It would be better to sort the names by **Surname** and **Initial**. Click in the **Sort** row of **Initials**, and specify **Ascending**. Do the same in the **Surname** column.

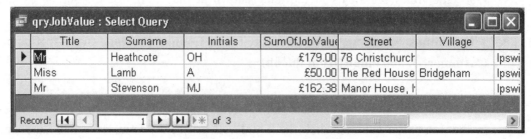

Figure 16.3: Query results

- Test your query again. It may not work quite correctly if the **Initials** field precedes the **Surname** field, because **Initials** is used as the first sort field rather than **Surname**. To correct this, you need to switch the two columns in the query.

- In **Design View**, click just above the **Surname** column title to select the column. Then click again in the same spot, holding the mouse button down and dragging to the left of **Initials**.

- Test your query again and if all is well, save it, giving it the title *qryJobValue*.

Step 2: Creating a report from the query

Nothing new here; the report can be created using a wizard, and the fields moved around as required. The final report should look something like Figure 16.4.

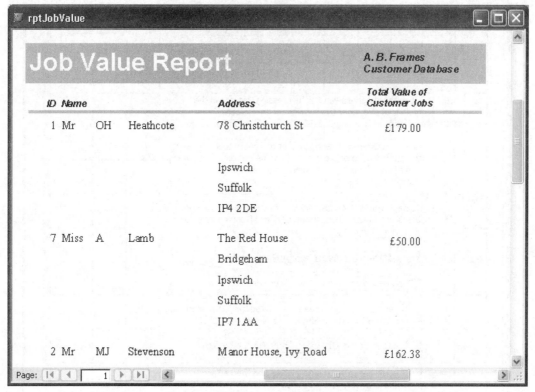

Figure 16.4: The rptJobValue report

Performing the mail merge

In Chapter 12 (Prototyping), we took a look at how to create a standard letter in Word, opened directly from Access using the OfficeLinks tool. For the finished application, a different letter will have to be created to match each set of customers for which a query has been created, since each letter uses a different data source. It is also possible that the users, once they become more confident in using the system, may want to create a completely new query and a standard letter to the new selection of customers.

In order to give them the flexibility to do this, but at the same time provide some guidance, the system design specifies that when the user selects the **Mail Merge** option from the menu, a form will open up with clear instructions displayed.

Create a blank form with Mail Merge instructions

- From the database window, click the **Forms** tab and then click **New**.

- In the **New Form** dialogue box, select **Design View** and leave the **table or query** list box empty. Click **OK**. An empty form will be created. We are aiming to make it look something like Figure 16.5.

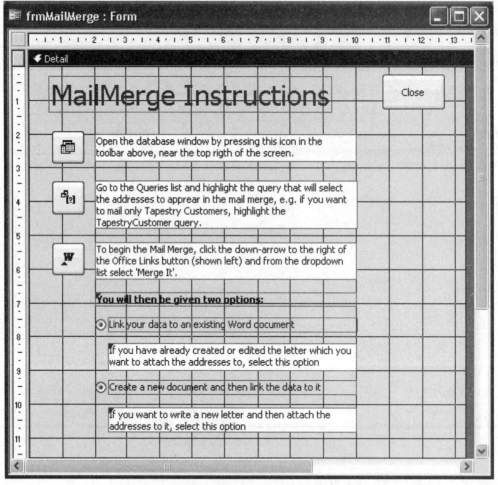

Figure 16.5: Mail merge instructions form

- Place a heading on the form by clicking the **Label** tool and then clicking and dragging at the top of the form. Adjust type size and font as required.

- Make sure the **Control Wizards** tool is deselected and click the **Command Button** tool. Click in the form.

- Now put a picture of the database window tool on the button, by altering its **Picture** property. Right-click the new button and open its property sheet.

- Click the **Picture** property, then the **Build** button.

- The complete list of bitmap images appears in the **Picture Builder** as shown in Figure 16.6. Select **Database Window**. Some of the icons may not be available, but this won't matter so long as the instructions are still clear.

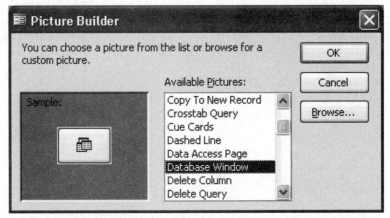

Figure 16.6: Placing a bitmap library picture on a command button

- Finish off the form by placing text and buttons as required. The **Close** button is created using the **Control Wizard**, and simply closes the form.

- Test the instructions for the **Mail Merge**. You may find that a second version of Access is opened up. The only course of action after displaying or printing the letters is to close Word and Access and then start up again.

Making the Main Menu load automatically

You may like to automatically load the main menu or a title screen as soon as the user opens the database. You do this with the **Startup** command.

- Make sure you have created a main menu form, even if it just consists of a blank form with a heading "Main Menu".

- On the **Tools** menu, click **Startup...** The **Startup** dialogue box appears.

- In the **Display Form/Page** box, click the dropdown arrow, and then select your Main Menu form (**fmnuMain**).

Next time you open your database, the main menu will appear automatically.

Note: The main menu for the final system is shown in Part 3. It is different from the one originally specified for the prototype solution in Figure 11.2 on page 93.

Adding a password

This is often impossible on a school or college network as it interferes with user privileges. On your computer at home, however, you can try it (although you should remove the password on any version you intend to use to demonstrate at your school or college).

- To set a password on the database, select **Tools**, **Security**, **Set Database Password…**
- Set it to **ABFrames**.

If you forget your password, you will never be able to edit or use your application again.

Chapter 17 – Debugging Aids

Objectives

By the end of this chapter you will have learned how to:

monitor variables;

step through code a line at a time;

set a breakpoint to stop running code;

use a message box for debugging purposes.

Types of error

 If you have done any programming, you will know that there are several types of error, including syntax errors, logic errors and run-time errors. When you write Visual Basic modules, you would be well advised to compile each module using the **Compile** tool, which will point out any syntax errors in your statements right away. (It is not strictly necessary to compile the modules in this way, because Access will automatically do this before running a module, but it saves time to check the syntax and correct errors before attempting to run the code.)

Run-time errors could be caused, for example, by not having a form open that is referred to in another module. Access displays an error message when this occurs and the cause is generally easy to trace.

Logic errors are the trickiest to find and correct, and Access provides a number of ways to help debug your code.

Using the Immediate window

When you have written a module and tested it, only to find it doesn't work, Access provides several ways for you to have a closer look at exactly what is going on. One way is to display the value of chosen controls or variables in the Immediate (Debug) window. To try this out, we'll use the code attached to the **On Open** event of the Job Sheet.

- Open the **frmCustomer** form in **Form View** and double-click a **JobNo** for one of the customers, which should open **frmJobSheet**, showing details of the selected job.

- Switch to **Design View** and click the right mouse button at the top left intersection of the ruler lines to display the popup menu. Select **Properties** to open the property sheet for the form.

- Click in the **On Open** event property and click the **Build** button (**...**) to display the **Module** window.

- Select **Immediate Window** from the **View** menu at the top of the screen.

- Move the **Debug** (it's easier to call it this than *Immediate*) window to the lower right corner of the screen, out of the way of the code in the **Module** window.

- You can use the **Debug** window to display the value of any control or variable. In the **Debug** window, type

- ?DisplayJob

-     and press **Enter** (see Figure 17.1)

- The value of the variable **DisplayJob** is displayed as *True*.

- Note that the question mark is shorthand for the **Print** statement; you could equally have typed

      ```
      Print DisplayJob
      ```

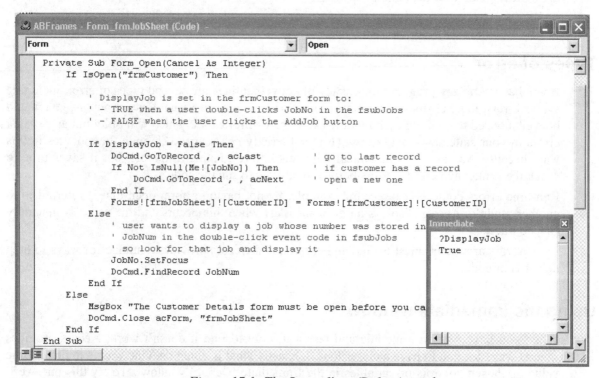

*Figure 17.1: The **Immediate (Debug)** window*

Setting a breakpoint to stop running code

Sometimes it is helpful to watch your code running. You can do this by setting a breakpoint in the code so that when it runs in the normal way, it stops at the breakpoint and the module window is displayed.

- Place the cursor in the first line of the procedure:

      ```
      If IsOpen("frmCustomer") Then
      ```

- In the **Debug** toolbar, click the **Breakpoint** button (or, alternatively, press the shortcut key **F9**). Both these are *toggles*, alternately setting and removing a breakpoint.

- Close the code window, and close the **frmJobSheet** form.

- In the **frmCustomer** form, double-click a **JobNo** to test the breakpoint in the **On Open** event of the **frmJobSheet**. The **Module** window opens, with the first line of the procedure highlighted. The **Debug** window will still be open too, unless you closed it earlier.

Stepping through code line by line

You can now step through the code one line at a time, to see exactly what sequence the instructions are executed in.

- Select **Step Into** from the **Debug** menu.

- Since the line just executed is a call to the function **IsOpen**, the next line to be executed is the first line of this function, so you will see the function displayed on your screen.

```
Public Function IsOpen(ByVal StrFormName As String) As Boolean
' Returns true if the specified form is open in form view
```

- Keep pressing the **Step Into** button (or the function key **F8**) and you will see one line at a time being executed. You can stop at any time, and display the value of anything you want to examine in the **Debug** window.

Stepping over procedures

Sometimes you don't want to bother stepping through functions, such as **IsOpen**, which are called by your own procedures. In that case, use the **Step Over** tool (or **Shift-F8**) instead of the **Step Into** tool.

- Close the Module window, leaving the breakpoint set.

- You can't run the code attached to an event procedure except by causing the event to occur, so close **frmJobSheet** and once again double-click a job in the **frmCustomer** form – or you could press the **Add Job** button, which will also open the Job Sheet.

- The module window will open. This time, select **Step Over** from the **Debug** menu.

- The code performs the function **IsOpen** without stepping through it a line at a time.

- Display the value **IsOpen("frmCustomer")** in the **Debug** window by typing

```
? IsOpen("frmCustomer")
```

It should return **True**.

- Remove the breakpoint by clicking in the breakpoint line and pressing **F9**.

Using a message box to display variables

Sometimes it is convenient to know what values have been assigned to certain variables without having to manually step through the code. One way of doing this is to insert an extra line of code in the module, which will display a message box showing the variable you are interested in.

- Just before the line **JobNo.SetFocus**, add the following line of code:

```
MsgBox "JobNo and JobNum are currently " & JobNo & "   " & JobNum
```

- Save the code, close the **frmJobSheet** form, and test the message box by double-clicking a job number in the **frmCustomer** form. The message box is displayed as soon as the form opens, as shown in Figure 17.2.

Figure 17.2: A temporary message box

- Click **OK**.

- Switch to **Design View**, open the code window and delete (or comment out) the **MsgBox** instruction.

Chapter 18 – Testing

Testing objectives

Your test strategy should be included in the Design section of your report. In addition, your project should include a section on testing: the test data, the test plan, how it was carried out and what the results were. But what is the *purpose* of testing? It may seem obvious that it is to prove that the system works correctly.

In fact, you will formulate a much better test plan if you turn this idea on its head and consider the following rules, proposed by Glen Myers in his book *The Art of Software Testing*.

1. **Testing is a process of executing a program with the intent of finding an error.**

2. **A good test case is one that has a high probability of finding an as yet undiscovered error.**

3. **A successful test is one that uncovers an as yet undiscovered error.**

In other words, it is not sufficient to think up a few tests which you are fairly sure will not make your program crash or give a wrong result; you must use tests and test data which have been carefully thought out to test all parts of the program. How many times does a lecturer spend only a few minutes testing a project before it does something unexpected, to baffled cries of 'It's never done that before...' from the crestfallen student! This should never happen with a properly tested system.

Designing a test plan

Your test strategy should be included in the Design section of your project. This means planning how you are going to ensure that each module works as it should, that the modules still work correctly when they are all put together, and that all parts of the system are present and giving the expected results for all valid and invalid input and under all conditions.

Typically you will start by adding several records at the prototype stage, and testing basic functions such as updating and deleting records, attempting to add invalid data and so on. Performing these tests will very likely give you more ideas for validations, and other improvements you can make to the system. Have a paper and pencil handy and jot these ideas down, as well as the tests that you will need to perform to ensure that new modules and validations work correctly, and the expected results. These will then form part of your final test plan.

When the whole system is finished you will have to run through each of these tests again to make sure everything still works as expected. You would be surprised how often modules that worked perfectly last week no longer work, because of a change you have made elsewhere in the system.

Testing is a time-consuming, nit-picking business, requiring much imagination and patience. Remember that you are trying to uncover errors, not cover them up!

Steps in software testing

1.   Module testing

As you complete each module of your program, it needs to be thoroughly tested. Even if you can't test every combination of execution paths, you can test the important paths, the extreme cases, valid and invalid data, and so on. For the purposes of your project, you should aim to demonstrate that you have tested systematically and that your testing is *reasonably* exhaustive. A maximum of 20 to 30 pages of actual test runs which cover major processes and show a variety of test data (i.e. extreme, correct, incorrect) is quite sufficient.

Remember to test:

♦ all computations in the module

♦ correct termination of all loops

♦ valid and invalid input data

♦ 'exception' data, which will make the module follow a different execution path.

2.   System testing

When all the modules have been written and the whole system put together, system testing can begin.

At this stage, you should ideally test your system with a realistic volume of data. If the system is designed to hold details of 5000 stock items, and you have never tested it with more than 8, there is no way of knowing how it will perform after installation, unless you test it. Obviously, you will not have the time to enter 5000 different records, and the AQA recommendation is to enter about 50 records as a sufficient demonstration of a working system's ability to handle larger volumes of data.

Drawing up a test plan

The test plan should include a minimal set of test data and expected results for typical data and erroneous/extreme data.

For the module testing, draw up a test plan of preferably no more than two or three pages, which shows that you have chosen your test data carefully, tested each module, and know what the results ought to be. A good test plan for the sample project can be seen at the end of the Design section in Part 3. The headings used are slightly different from those given in the blank form for your use at the end of the book – there is no single correct format, so make your choice!

Test No	Test Data	Purpose	Expected Result	Comment/Verified
1	Enter incorrect password 'ABC'	Test password	Only password "ABF" accepted	
2	Enter CustomerID abc	Test invalid digits	Not accepted	

Sometimes it is impossible to show evidence that a test works correctly; in those cases, have your supervisor carry out the test and authenticate the result in the 'Comments/Verified' column. You could also use this column to reference the page number on which your test evidence is shown, or to make notes to yourself of any tests that did not work correctly.

Selecting tests for the test plan

Try to choose tests that test the more complex aspects of your system, such as calculations, command buttons that perform updating or open up a form with data already in it, and so on. Masses of tests for really trivial validations that are performed automatically by Access (such as a date in the correct format) are fairly pointless.

You may well have to amend or add to your initial test plan as the program develops, but you will find it very helpful to have a written plan at all stages, even if you keep adjusting it.

Similarly, if you design your system tests **before** you start coding, you will be forced to think about how this phase will be carried out, what will have to be done to make system testing possible, and how to ensure that it will be successful. The earlier you can foresee any problems, the easier they will be to solve.

Presenting the test results

Your test results should be presented in an appendix, and cross-referenced to your test plan. They will normally take the form of test runs, screen dumps and file dumps. You may need to explain exactly what data was used as input. Use a highlighter pen to emphasise the key point about a screenshot, and annotate the output by hand to show what the test proves. Be selective, and consider it a challenge to make it as easy as possible for a reader to confirm that test results were as expected. As a general rule, include the absolute minimum information needed to get the point across.

Test runs and screenshots with no annotation and no cross-referencing to the test plan are virtually useless!

For a large project with a correspondingly large number of tests, it would be sufficient to include samples of the test output and screenshots, and have the rest of the tests authenticated by your supervisor. There is no need to include hundreds of pages of screenshots.

Chapter 19 – The Report

Objectives

By the end of this chapter you will have learned how to document your project.
It should include:

A title page;

A table of contents;

Sections on:

> Analysis,
>
> Design,
>
> Testing,
>
> Systems maintenance (technical) manual,
>
> User manual,
>
> An appraisal of the project;

Appendices showing for example:

> input documents,
>
> annotated program listings,
>
> test runs, annotated and cross-referenced to test plan.

Introduction

The report that you hand in at the end of your project contains all the evidence of the work you have done over the past few months. No matter how careful your analysis, how appropriate the design, how clever the programming and how thorough the testing; if the written evidence is not there to prove it, you will not achieve a good mark.

It will take longer than you expect to complete the documentation. It will pay you to write the documentation in parallel with the other stages of the project and not leave it all to the end. Then, when you have finished the implementation and testing, you will be able to go through it all, proof reading, adding a table of contents, page numbers, and appendices.

Should the documentation be wordprocessed?

The short answer is *yes*. It should also be thoroughly spellchecked, both using the spellchecking facility provided by the wordprocessor, and by reading it through slowly and carefully. Remember that a spellchecker won't find misspellings like *the* instead of *then*, or even *curser* instead of *cursor*, as the manuals of one software firm will testify!

Wordprocessing skills

There are some crucial wordprocessing skills which you need to acquire in order to present a really professional-looking final report. This document must do justice to the effort you have so far put into your project; it is all that the examiner will see, and even if you feel you have perhaps not achieved as much as you could have, a well-presented report will help.

Use the MS Word help system to learn new skills, including:

♦ **Setting styles for the various level of headings and text in your document.** The **Normal** template comes with built-in styles for **Heading 1**, **Heading 2**, **Heading 3** and **Normal** text. You may like to alter the font, size, style and justification of these, or set up new styles of your own.

♦ **Creating a Table of Contents.** If you have used styles consistently throughout your document, you can create a table of contents automatically. Put your cursor where you want the table of contents to appear, select **Insert**, **Reference**, **Index and Tables...** from the menu and then **Table of Contents**. It can be updated at any time by selecting it and pressing **F9**.

♦ **Inserting headers and footers.** The project title and the page number can be placed in either a header or footer. Select **View**, **Header and Footer** from the menu bar.

♦ **Inserting a page break whenever you want one.** Press **Ctrl-Enter**.

♦ **Using numbered points and bullet points.** Use the tools on the toolbar.

♦ **Creating tab stops.** Never use the space bar to indent; nothing will line up when you print the document. Learn to use the tab stops on the ruler line, and the **Tab** key (above **Caps Lock** on the keyboard) to tab.

♦ **Inserting tables.** Use the **Table** menu.

♦ **Inserting screenshots.** When you want to take a screenshot to include in your User Manual, for example, press **Alt-Print Screen** to copy the current window to the clipboard. Then switch to your Word document and use **Edit**, **Paste**. A better way is to use a screen capture utility program to copy your screens to a file, from where they can be linked to your document using **Insert**, **Picture**, **From File...**

How long should the documentation be?

Basically, it will have to be as many pages as it takes to do the job properly. The AQA guidelines suggest that project reports should not exceed 4000 words, with listings and test runs being added as appendices.

The guideline of 4000 words is designed to give you an idea of the size and scope of project that is expected at this level. You must be selective in what you include and avoid duplicating information; if you have included a systems flowchart in the Design section, for example, there is no need to reproduce it in the Systems Maintenance section. Just refer the reader to the relevant page.

Putting it all together

Your project documentation should be neatly bound in such a manner that it can be read without a major unbinding job. A ring binder is too large and heavy to be conveniently posted, so investigate the shelves of your local stationery shop to find something suitable.

Do not put each page (or several pages together) in a plastic sleeve; it makes the project report heavy, expensive to post, and inconvenient for marking.

Title page

The title page should include the title of the project, your name and centre, school or college. It could also include the date you submitted the project and your candidate number, if appropriate.

Table of contents

This is a must. Include in it the sections and numbered subsections, together with page numbers. Every page in your project should be numbered for easy reference; you can add page numbers by hand at the end to pages of test data, for example.

Analysis

A suggested framework for the Analysis section is given at the end of Chapter 10. Remember to include a write-up of your preparation for the interview (such as a list of questions), and a summary of the main points gleaned during the interview. Do not include a transcript of the interview. A questionnaire, if you have used one, can be included, together with a summary of responses. Your own observations of the current system, and deductions, are worth including also. If your analysis included, for example, reading about other similar systems, or trying out other similar software packages, then that can be written up here.

Design

Chapter 11 discusses what should be in your Design section; make sure you have covered all aspects of the design in your documentation. Your test strategy should be included in this section. You must aim to show that you have worked out what tests need to be performed and what results you expect. If you number the tests, it will make it easier to cross reference them to the actual test runs.

Testing

Testing is a vitally important part of the project. The test data and test plan should be included in this section. The Testing section should also contain a *test plan analysis* to show that it does test all parts of the system. Then, in the Systems Maintenance section, you can refer to any unusual results or unsolved problems.

Test runs may be included in an appendix. **The test runs should be cross-referenced clearly to the test plan,** and be presented in such a way that the reader can see at once what a specific page of output is designed to show. Devising appropriate tests, organising and cross-referencing screen dumps and printed output can take a great deal of time and ingenuity. There is no point including several pages of output with no explanation of what test it relates to or how the output proves that a certain section of the program is working correctly. Make handwritten annotations on the output and use highlighter pen to show significant results.

There is a great temptation to skimp on this section of the project; the feeling is 'Right! I've finished the programming and I'm pretty sure it all works. Here's a disk – you try it...'. Unfortunately, the devising and implementation of the test plan is *your* job, not the examiner's!

System maintenance

This section is aimed at a programmer who would be maintaining or enhancing the system. It could include the following:

1. Schematic diagrams summarising how modules relate to each other (or a reference to diagrams already included in the design section).

2a. Where a program or suite of programs has been written, for each module in the system:
  ♦ a brief description
  ♦ module name
  ♦ modules called up
  ♦ calling modules
  ♦ variables list – with type, purpose, format and example content
  ♦ high level pseudocode or flowchart.

2b. Where a package has been used:
  ♦ a brief description of each object in the system, i.e. form, report, query, module.
  ♦ a summary of the purpose of each macro or module, and when it is used
  ♦ high level pseudocode or flowchart for each module
  ♦ an explanation of the features you have used, and a description of how you tailored the package to suit the user's requirements.

3. Limitations of the system.

4. Discussion of unresolved problems or odd test results.

5. Special operational details.

6. You will also be awarded marks in this section for program code, if your project has involved writing a program, macros, SQL or other code as part of the customisation of a software package. The listing should be a genuine printout rather than a wordprocessed document, and should be clearly annotated by hand wherever this helps to explain what is happening. It needs to be made easily understandable, for example by:
  ♦ using meaningful variable names
  ♦ stating the purpose of each variable unless it is self-explanatory
  ♦ using comments to state the purpose of each procedure
  ♦ using comments, where necessary, to explain the logic of a particular section
  ♦ grouping procedures in a logical order so that it is easy to find your way around a long program
  ♦ using indentation to clarify the extent of loops and condition statements
  ♦ using blank lines between procedures to separate them.

System-generated code such as that produced by wizards or recorded macros should be clearly labelled as such.

User manual

This section is aimed entirely at a non-technical user and should use ordinary English rather than 'computer-speak'. For example, do not say 'Boot up the system' when 'Switch on the computer' will achieve the same result.

Presentation is all-important here. Use whatever facilities your wordprocessor has to enhance the appearance of the document, spellcheck it carefully and read it through to make sure it flows well and makes sense. It should be a 'stand-alone' document and could even be bound separately from the rest of the project.

Your user manual should include:

♦ a table of contents

♦ an introduction, stating what the system is about and who it is for

♦ examples of actual screen displays such as menus, data input screens and output screens

♦ samples of printed output

♦ an explanation of what each option on a menu does

♦ any special instructions on how to input data – for example the format of a date field, or the range of accepted values in an amount field

♦ an explanation of any manual procedures such as batching or recording data manually

♦ error messages that may be displayed and what to do in that event

♦ error recovery procedures – for example what to do if you realise you have made a wrong data entry, or the power goes off in the middle of an update

If you have used a package, explain how to use the system you have created, rather than explaining how to use the software package in general terms. It is a good idea to test out your user manual on the user or a colleague to see if they can follow your instructions without any extra help from you.

Appraisal

Finally, your documentation should include a *critical appraisal* of the completed project. This should be clearly related to the list of specific objectives written in the Analysis section. The more clearly you have stated the objectives, the easier it will be to evaluate how well your system achieved them.

If the project has been written for a real user, it is a good idea to include the user's comments in this section, perhaps in the form of a letter written on official headed paper and signed by the user. If any suggestions have been made for amendment or improvement, include these as well, whether or not you have managed to incorporate the suggestions. Add your own suggestions for improvement and possibilities for future development. Do take note that a fake letter from your best friend or a glowing letter from an uncritical parent stating how marvellous your system is, flying in the face of all the evidence, is not likely to gain you any marks.

Be honest about the shortcomings of the project; if it is not complete, maybe this is because it was over-ambitious and you should say so. You will not, however, score many marks for criticising the hardware, software, staff or lack of time. One of the skills to be learned in writing a project is to finish it on time in spite of all the difficulties you may encounter.

Part 3

Specimen Project

Customer Database

'A' Level Computing
Project

Submitted by:

A. Student (Candidate Number 543)

Any College (Centre Number 67890)

March 2004

Table of Contents

Section 1 - Analysis

1. Introduction

Create and use styles for section and paragraph headings. Then you will be able to automatically generate a table of contents. 12pt Times Roman, used in this report, is a good choice for body text.

A. B. Frames is a small privately-run business owned and run by Mr and Mrs Daniels. They specialise in selling works of art such as paintings and prints by local artists, and restoring and framing pictures, photographs, tapestries and so on. They have built up a large customer base and this is increasing every year.

Sales are boosted by holding regular exhibitions of paintings by various artists to which regular customers are invited as well as being advertised locally. Although the Daniels do hold a list of customers on a DOS-based filing system, they have no means of targeting customers who are likely to be interested in a particular exhibition, and automatically sending them invitations.

You must include an introduction. Background information about the business or organisation can be described if relevant. Then give an overview of what the project is about.

Mr and Mrs Daniels have decided to invest in a comprehensive customer information system to hold details of who their customers are, what orders or purchases they have made in the past, what their particular interests are and whether they attend exhibitions, so that they can offer their customers a better and more personalised service, save money on unproductive mailshots to the wrong customers, and boost sales by sending details of special offers, exhibitions, etc. to carefully selected customers.

2. The investigation

Preparing for the interview

An interview with Mrs Daniels was arranged and a list of topics for discussion drawn up prior to the interview. These included:

♦ the precise objectives of the new system;

♦ the problems or weaknesses in the current DOS system and the manual system;

♦ the methods currently used to record data;

♦ the information that needs to be kept on each customer;

♦ the required output;

♦ the volume of data (e.g., the number of existing customers, the number of new customers each month/year);

♦ any hardware or software constraints—e.g., did they already have hardware or software which they proposed to use?

Summary of the interview

You are not encouraged to include an actual transcript of the interview; just give a summary of the information you gained.

A number of weaknesses in the current manual system and DOS file system came to light during the interview, and some new objectives were stated. These are discussed below.

Mrs Daniels has recently purchased a Pentium PC running Windows XP, and a laser printer. She has also purchased, on the recommendation of a friend, the Microsoft Office suite including MS Access. Her original idea was that she should learn how to use Access and develop the system herself, but having spent some time with an Access textbook realised that the task is more complex than she at first realised and would be simply too time-consuming.

There are about 500 regular customers on the old DOS system, with about 30 new customers being added every year.

3. Problems with the current system

i) Tracing previous orders placed by a customer

In your project, include sample input and output documents from the current system in an appendix.

Each time a customer comes in to buy something or have a painting framed or restored, a job sheet is completed. The customer is given one copy, and the other copy is filed. (*An example is shown in Part 2, Figure 10.1.*) Frequently, a customer will come back several months later and ask, for example, for another tapestry to be framed 'using the same sort of frame as last time'. This means a lengthy search through hundreds of job sheets, and often the relevant one cannot be located.

ii) Inability to send targeted mailshots

The current DOS filing system does not hold any details on customers' particular interests or what past purchases they have. Currently it is not possible to send out a mailshot to only selected customers, although labels can be printed to all customers in the database. With the number of customers increasing every year, this is impractical and expensive.

iii) Lack of information about customer base

There is a general lack of information about who the most frequent customers are, who has not made any purchases for the past few years, what the most popular items are, etc. Access to summarised information of this kind could be useful for planning future stock purchases, marketing campaigns and so on.

4. Objectives of the new system

This is one of the most important paragraphs in the report! If you identify and state the objectives clearly, the design and appraisal will be very much easier.

The objectives may be stated in both quantitative and qualitative terms.

1. It should take less than 30 seconds to establish whether a customer is already on file.

2. It should be possible to go directly from the Customer Details screen to the entry of a job for that customer, without having to re-enter the customer's name, etc.

3. Data entry should be as fast and easy as possible, particularly as there are several hundred existing customers and jobs to be entered when the system is first installed.

4. It should take less than one minute to trace any past job for a customer.

5. There must be provision for multi-item jobs; for example a job could consist of the **restoration** and **framing** of a picture.

6. The new system is required to provide the following information:

   ♦ a list of all business customers;

   ♦ a list of all customers interested in a given artist or given subject matter, or who are classified as 'Tapestry', 'Restoration' 'Framing' or 'Exhibition' customers;

   ♦ a list of all customers whose total jobs exceed a given value.

7. It should be possible to send a standard letter to selected customers, using criteria mentioned above.

8. The user must be able to create new letters whenever needed and perform a mail merge to selected customers.

9. The main menu should be displayed automatically when the database is loaded, and the whole system should be menu-driven.

5. Data flows

A data flow diagram of the proposed system is shown below:

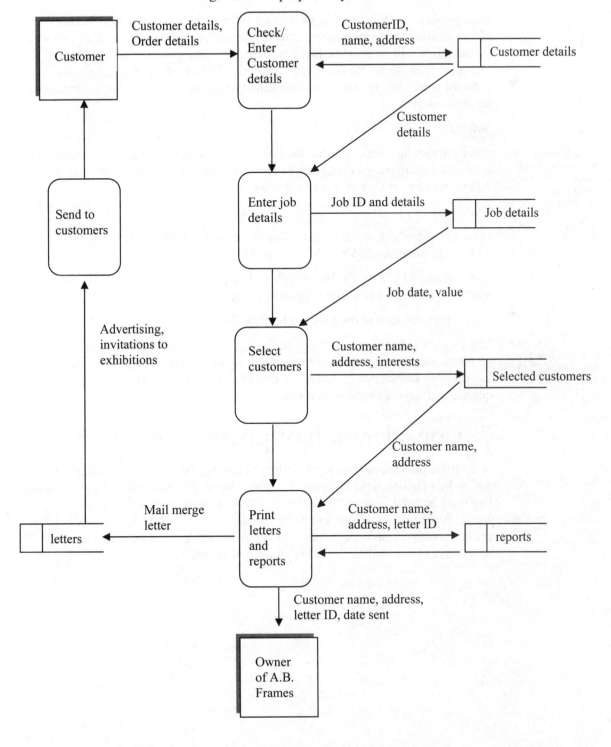

6. Constraints and limitations

System boundaries (scope of proposed system)

The system to be developed is a customer information system, and is intended to enhance rather than replace the current system of recording jobs. If this proves successful, it will be possible at a future date to replace the current method of recording jobs so that the details are typed directly into the computer and the required copies printed out. This could then be extended to link into a computerised accounts system.

Software

Specify the details of the hardware and software that will be used both for development and by the user, including the version number

The customer has requested that the system be developed using MS Access 2003, so unless a good reason transpires for using an alternative program or package, Access will be the first choice of software.

Hardware

In order to run Access 2003 and be able to perform a mail merge using Word, a PC with a minimum of 128Mb will be required.

The user has a PC with 128Mb, which will be perfectly suitable, and similar machines are available for development work at the College.

User's level of information technology skills

The user's I.T. skills may be a relevant factor in the design of the system

Mrs Daniels is familiar with Word and has good keyboard skills, so should have no problem entering data and learning how to use the system. She would like to improve her knowledge of Access so that she can, in the future, perform new queries and reports as the need arises.

7. Consideration of possible solutions

The AQA requires 'A' level candidates to assess the feasibility of potential solutions and justify the chosen one.

A database package will be ideal for implementing the system for A. B. Frames, and as Mrs Daniels has requested that it be done in Access 2003, this is the package that must be used. It would probably be possible to implement the system using Visual Basic or another programming language but it would take a lot longer and could possibly involve the owners having to buy more software which is not really necessary, as Access has all the capabilities required.

I already have some experience of Access 2003 and it is available both at home and at College for development.

Using this package it will be possible to:

♦ set up the necessary tables and relationships;

♦ produce customised input screens, using Visual Basic to automate data entry wherever possible and to perform various validations;

♦ use Visual Basic modules to enable fast searches foe a particular customer and past jobs;

♦ design reports as needed;

♦ make and save queries to select certain customers for a mail merge;

♦ link with MS Word to enable new letters to be composed and to perform mail merges to selected customers;

♦ implement a customised menu system.

Assessment

The Analysis gives a clear outline for a problem of adequate scope. Details of the research are evident but more details on the type of output required and the current data sources, destinations and processes would have been useful. This could have been set out in a DfD of the current system together with a preliminary data dictionary. There are clear objectives but perhaps more consideration should have been given to the type of Management Information that Mrs Daniels required e.g. information about customers who have not purchased anything recently. (Objective 6 could really do with expanding) There are good reasons given for the use of Access but scant consideration of other possible solutions.

Section 2 - Design

1. Overall system design

The input, processes, database tables and output are shown in the following system outline chart.

INPUT	PROCESSES

Customer Details:
    ID, Name, Address, Tel,
    Customer type, Business
    Customer (Y/N), Notes
 	
Job (Order) Details:
    JobNo, Customer ID,
    Order date, Order value,
    Number of items in job
 	
For each line of job order:
 	
    Item type (Sales,
Framing
        etc), Artist name if
    picture, Description,
    Frame, Cost
	Add, edit, delete customers
	
	Add, edit, delete job orders
	
	Look up all jobs for a customer
	
	Print out reports:
	    All business customers
	    Customers who have purchased work by
	     a particular artist
	    Customers who have attended
	     exhibitions
	
	Mail merge to selected customers

TABLES	**OUTPUT**

Customer table
 	
Job table
 	
Order Line (Job Item) table
	Display: Jobs for a customer
	
	Reports:
	    All business customers
	    Customers who have purchased work
	    by a particular artist
	    Customers who have
	    attended exhibitions etc.
	
	    Mail merge letters

2. Database design

The database contains three entities: CUSTOMER, JOB and ITEM. These are related as follows:

An entity-relationship diagram such as this one is essential as part of the database design.

Tables will be created for each of these entities.

3. Definition of data requirements

Document the type and length of each attribute carefully, BEFORE you start work in Access. Discrepancies in the type and length of foreign key fields in different tables can cause major problems later on

The tables will contain the following data:

tblCustomer

Attribute Name	Comments	Data Type and Length	Validation
CustomerID*	Automatically incremented	Long Integer	Unique primary key
Title		Text (4)	
Surname		Text (25)	
Initials	Automatically converted to uppercase	Text (3)	
Street		Text (30)	
Village		Text (30)	
Town		Text (30)	Default to Ipswich
County		Text (20)	Default to Suffolk
PostCode	Automatically converted to uppercase	Text (10)	
HomeTelephone		Text (15)	
WorkTelephone		Text (20)	
SalesCustomer		Yes/No	
FramingCustomer		Yes/No	
RestorationCustomer		Yes/No	
TapestryCustomer		Yes/No	
ExhibitionCustomer		Yes/No	
BusinessCustomer		Yes/No	
BusinessName	Skipped if not business customer	Text	
CustomerNotes		Memo	

tblJob

Attribute Name	Comments	Data Type	Validation
JobNo*		Long Integer	Unique primary key
CustomerID		Integer	Must exist on tblCustomer table
Orderdate		Date	Must be a valid date
JobValue	Total of individual item values	Currency	(Automatically calculated)
ItemsInJob	The number of items on this Job sheet	Integer	(Automatically calculated)
JobNotes		Memo	

tblItem

Attribute Name	Comments	Data Type and length	Validation
ItemNo*	1,2, etc., for items in Job	Long Integer	Must be numeric and unique
JobNo*	ItemNo and JobNo constitute the unique primary key	Integer	Must exist on tblJob table
ItemType	Will cause the check box on frmCustomer form to be automatically set	Text (11)	Must be one of Sales, Framing, Exhibition, Tapestry or Restoration (Selected from list box)
ArtistName		Text (20)	Selected from combo box
SubjectMatter	Description of painting sold, e.g. Dogs, Portrait, Suffolk Landscape	Text (20)	selected from combo box
ItemValue	Price charged for Sale/Job	Currency	
ItemDescription		Text (30)	
Frame	Type and/or colour of frame	Text (20)	

4. Design of input forms

Two data entry forms are needed.

1.   frmCustomer

This form will be used for several purposes so it needs facilities to:

♦ check to see whether a customer is already on the database;

♦ add a new customer;

♦ move to the frmJobSheet form to enter a new job for the current customer;

♦ look through all the existing jobs for the current customer and bring up more details if necessary.

Look at any specimen input documents to see if certain default values would be appropriate.

Validations will be performed automatically. The CustomerID field will be an integer field and will automatically increment when a new customer is added, to ensure a unique ID without the user having to know what the last ID used was. Wherever possible, default values will be inserted automatically (e.g., most customers are from Ipswich, Suffolk, so the relevant fields will default to those values). Tab order will also be used to speed data entry; e.g. if Business Customer is not checked, the field for Business Name will be automatically skipped.

In order to look up details for a particular job, the Job Number field in the subform can be double-clicked to automatically bring up the Job Sheet.

The frmCustomer form will be as shown on the next page.

2.   frmJobSheet

This form will be accessible only from (1) the frmCustomer form when the Add Job button is pressed, or (2) a JobNo on the frmCustomer form is double-clicked as explained above.

The frmJobSheet form will be as shown on the next page.

CUSTOMER DETAILS FORM

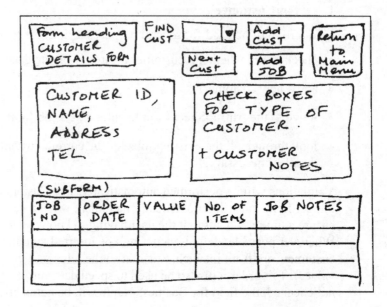

Hand-drawn screen layouts are preferable to screenshots of your final screens. These should be drawn BEFORE you start work at the computer

JOB SHEET

| Form heading "JOB SHEET" | DELETE JOB | RETURN TO CUSTOMER DETAILS |

JOB ID [   ]   DATE [   ]

| CUSTOMER DETAILS (ALREADY DISPLAYED ON FORM) | JOB NOTES |

JOB NO	ITEM NO	ITEM TYPE	SUBJECT	etc
	1			

JOB VALUE [   ]   No of Items [   ]

CALCULATED AUTOMATICALLY

Alternatively, you could print out the screen as produced automatically by a wizard, and annotate it by hand to show how you intend to customise it.

5. Report design

The format of all the reports will be similar. The layout of the rptBusinessCustomer report is shown below:

It would be better to show a hand-drawn design for a proposed report. It is not necessary to use squared paper and lay out every character; simply show what headings you will use, what data will appear and in approximately what position.

A.B Frames Ltd
Customer Database

Business Customer Report

ID	Name	Address	Home Telephone
			Work Telephone
16	Mr D Grieves	19 Church St	567890
		Ipswich	453210
		Suffolk	
		IP7 5GF	
576	Mrs P Mason	34 Kipling St	745221
		Ipswich	01728-998766
		Suffolk	
		IP6 4ER	

6. Mail merge

The Mail Merge option will allow the user to load up Word directly from Access, and specify which of several queries is to be used as the source of the data. The user is given the option to use an existing letter or create a new letter. This feature is not to be totally automated, as the users wish to have the flexibility to create new letters themselves, and possibly even to create new queries when they become more confident in the use of the system.

When Mail Merge is selected on the menu, instructions on how to proceed will appear on screen.

Emphasise user involvement throughout.

After discussion with the user, it was decided not to produce mailing labels, as there was less work involved in using window envelopes.

In order to keep a record of which customers have been mailed and when, reports have been designed using the same queries as those used in the mail merge, so that a list can be printed out and filed after performing a mail merge.

7. Queries

Queries which pick out various categories of customer will be created and saved, as follows:

qryArtistName	Allows user to specify an artist's name, then selects all customers who have purchased a painting by that artist.
qryBusinessCustomer	Selects all business customers.
qryExhibitionCustomer	Selects all customers who have attended exhibitions.
qryFramingCustomer	Selects all customers who have had a framing job done.
qryJobValue	Allows the user to specify a currency amount and then selects all customers who have had total jobs exceeding that amount.
qryRestorationCustomer	Selects all customers who have had restoration work done.
qrySalesCustomer	Selects all customers who have bought paintings, etc.
qrySubjectMatter	Allows the user to type in a specific subject matter and selects all customers who have had jobs specifying that subject matter.
qryTapestryCustomer	Selects all customers who have had work done on tapestries.

8. Menu design

The menu structure is as follows:

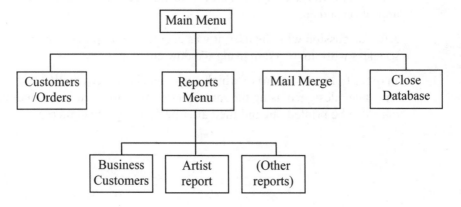

9. Systems flowchart

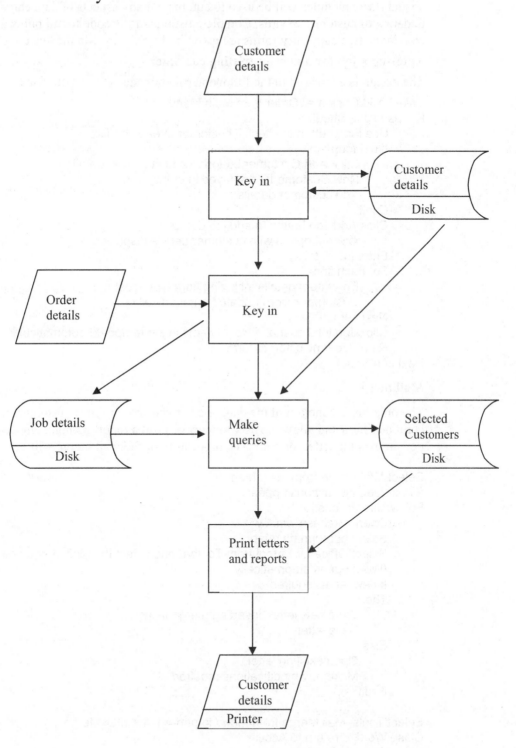

10. Module design

Visual Basic modules will be used to automate many aspects of data entry and updating of customer records. Complete listings of the code for all buttons, events, etc., in the two data entry forms are given in the Systems Maintenance section.

Entering a job for a new or existing customer

The design is expressed in the following pseudocode.

```
Select Add Customer/Order from Main Menu
For each Job Sheet:
        Use Find button to check if customer already on file
        If not found,
                Click Add Customer button to add customer details
                New CustomerID displayed in empty form
                Add customer details
        Endif
        Click Add Job button to add job details
        frmJobSheet opens with customer details displayed
        Enter job details
        For each item:
                Enter Item details including Item type, cost
                Customer record updated automatically
        Next item
        Click Job total cost and No. of items in job to update automatically
        Return to frmCustomer form
Next Job Sheet
```

Mail merge

The other main function of the database is to be able to select customers matching certain criteria and allow the user to view or print a report listing them, send them a new or existing letter, or both. The procedure for the mail merge will be:

```
Select Mail Merge from Main Menu
(On-screen instructions appear)
Follow instructions to
        Open database window
        Select appropriate query
        Select Office Links tool from Toolbar and select the Mail Merge option
        (Word opens automatically)
        If new letter required
        Then
                Write new letter, inserting merge fields
                Save letter
        Else
                Open existing letter
                Make any modifications required
        Endif

Select Tools, Mail Merge from menu to perform the Mail Merge
Close Word to return to Access
Select Reports from Main Menu
Print report to have hard copy listing of which customers mailed
```

Show how the design is influenced by the user's requirements or level of I.T. skills

Although it would be possible for the system to incorporate a basic letter corresponding to each query (for a particular selection of customers), the user opted to have a less automated mail merge as the situation will inevitably arise when they want to make a new query and create a new letter. This will be much easier for them if they have already got used to the procedure for performing a mail merge from scratch.

11. Security

A password will be attached to the database so that it is only accessible to someone who knows the password. Different access levels are not needed, as Mr and Mrs Daniels are the only people who will be using the database.

12. Test strategy

The test strategy will include five different types of testing as described below.

Logical testing

You must describe an appropriate test strategy in the Design section. Put the detailed test plan and test results in the Testing section.

This will be used to test every aspect of each form, report and query as soon as it is implemented, using valid, invalid and extreme data. Test data will be added to test each code module and results compared with the expected results. Sufficient data will be added to ensure that there is at least one customer in each category (e.g. 'Tapestry Customer'). The test data that will be added initially is shown in Appendix 1. Subsequent tests will often involve adding new data which will then be deleted when the test works satisfactorily.

Functional testing

Each menu item will be tested in turn to ensure that no function has been missed out.

System testing

When the system is complete, the whole range of tests will be carried out again to ensure that no errors have been introduced.

Recovery testing

The computer will be rebooted while the database is open, to ensure that data is not lost or corrupted in the event of a power failure.

Acceptance testing

The user will then be involved and asked to test all the capabilities of the program to ensure that all required functions are present and working in the manner expected. This testing may result in further refinements.

Assessment

The Design section is clear and a third party could attempt to use the information to build the system.

The database design could have been extended to show the record structure together with an explanation why the structure given is in third normal form.

The I/O screens need to be annotated as to why the form is a good HCI, e.g. clear headings, Return buttons always in same place, etc.

The processes need to match the objectives.

The functional, system and user testing needs to be expanded to clearly match the framing system - e.g. would Mrs Daniels be booking in some customers' jobs?

Section 3 - Testing

1. Test plan

Test No.	Test	Expected result
1	Test password	Only "ABF" accepted. Main menu opens automatically.
2	Test Main menu option Customer/Orders	frmCustomer form opens.
3	Enter first customer	Automatically given CustomerID 1. Default values correctly inserted.
4	Enter customers 2 to 15	CustomerID incremented automatically, but can be changed by the user if required. Initials and post code capitalised automatically. Business name skipped if not business customer. Tab order correct throughout form.
5	Use Find Customer button to find Belles	Belles P located and displayed.
6	Use the Next button to find next customer named Belles	Belles FR located and displayed.
7	Press Next button again	Text on button changes to 'No More'.
8	Press Add Customer, then Add Job before entering customer name	Customised error message appears: 'Enter customer details before entering job'. Customer form remains open.
9	Press Add Customer, enter customer name, then press Add Job button	frmJobSheet opens with customer name displayed. Job can be entered.
10	Press 'Return to Customer Details'	Customer form opens showing the same customer and, in the subform, the job that was just added.

Test No.	Test	Expected result
11	For customer 23 (Zelter) add job 31, 1 item, type 'Restoration'	'Restoration' category automatically checked on frmCustomer, Job appears in subform.
12	For customer 23 add job 33, 1 item, type 'Framing'	'Framing' category automatically checked on frmCustomer, Job appears in subform.
13	For customer 23 add job 34, 1 item, type 'Tapestry'	'Tapestry' category automatically checked on frmCustomer, Job appears in subform.
14	For customer 23 add job 35, 1 item, type 'Exhibition'	'Exhibition' category automatically checked on frmCustomer, Job appears in subform.
15	For customer 23 add job 36, 1 item, type 'Sales'	'Sales' category automatically checked on frmCustomer, Job appears in subform.
16	For customer 2, add job 17 with 2 items: Framing (£50) and Sales (£75), total value £125	Job total and number of items correctly calculated, frmCustomer form correctly refreshed.
17	Add job 777 for Customer 1 (L.P. Heathcote), date 2/3/00 to test that date is correctly entered	Date recorded as 02/03/2000.
18	Attempt to add another job 777	An error message is displayed, and the new addition is unsuccessful.
19	Attempt to leave Job form without entering a job for Customer 1	JobNo 0 is saved on file.
20	Repeat previous test	Error message: Duplicate JobNo (because 2 jobs with ID 0).
21	In frmCustomer form locate Customer 1 and highlight and delete JobNo 0	Job deleted.

Test No.	Test	Expected result
22	Double-click JobNo 777 in frmCustomer form with Customer 1 (L.P.Heathcote) on screen	frmJobSheet form opens with details on screen.
23	Change Item 2 price from £0 to £20, and click in Total Price field	Total job price updated on Job Form and on frmCustomer form.
24	Print report of all business customers	All business customers appear on report.
25	Print rptArtist report, entering artist 'Constable' for artist name	All customers who have bought a work by Constable should appear on report.
26	Print rptJobValue report, specifying job value of £50	All customers with over £50 in jobs appear on report.
27	Select Mail Merge option	Mail merge instructions appear.
28	Test Mail Merge for Exhibition customers, creating a new letter, by following Mail Merge instructions	Letters to Hallet, Heathcote (FR), Heathcote (LP), Jones, Thomas, Williams and Zelter.
29	Test Mail Merge for Customers whose jobs total over £1000, using existing letter	Letters to L.P.Heathcote and O.H.Head.
30	Test Reports Menu option, then each submenu option	Reports correctly printed.
31	Test Return to Main Menu button on frmCustomer form	Main Menu appears.
32	Select Close Database	Access closes down.
33	Test 'recovery' after power failure	Only current changes lost.

About 30 tests should be sufficient; don't go overboard in a project with a limit on the recommended size.

2. Test results

You can include test results in an appendix. It is not necessary to put them into a word-processed document. Use hand annotation and highlighter pen to draw the reader's attention to the important points in the screenshot.

The test results for the final test run are shown below. Errors which came to light during earlier test runs were corrected and all tests gave expected results.

Test 1: test password

When the correct password was entered, the database opened. Otherwise, the following message was displayed:

Test 2. Enter first customer in empty database

CustomerID correctly set to 1

Test 3: Enter customers 2 to 15

Customer details entered. All different options, defaults and fields were tested during data entry. The tests resulted in some minor changes to field order, tab order, and default values to make data entry as smooth as possible. During user testing, the addition of a 'Delete Customer' button was discussed but rejected as the user is quite at ease with using the built-in Access 'Delete' button on the toolbar.

Test 4: Use Find Customer button to find Belles

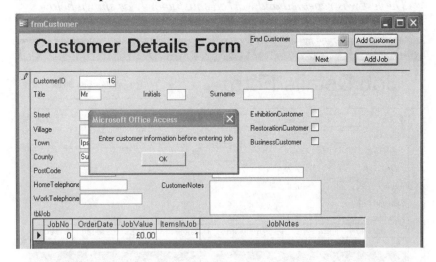

Record for 'Belles' is displayed when selected

Test 8: Attempt to add job before entering customer details

Comment: This test initially resulted in the frmJobSheet form opening with no customer details displayed, which would have left a job on the file for an unknown customer if the user had not noticed that they had forgotten to enter at least the customer's name. The message appears if the surname field is left empty when Add Job is pressed.

Test 9: Add customer name only, and then press Add Job

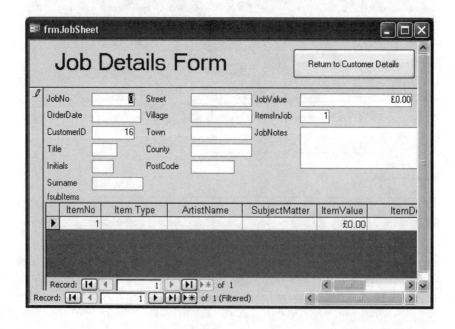

*Comment: This was an unexpected result when changing focus to the fsubItems subform: the customer details had not been saved by Access prior to opening the Job Sheet. The problem was fixed by inserting a line of code **Me.Refresh** in the module attached to the 'Add Job' button on the customer sheet.*

The test was repeated and worked satisfactorily as shown below.

In cases where it is difficult to show evidence that the test worked correctly, you could ask your teacher/lecturer to perform the test and sign it off.

Test 10: Press 'Return to Customer' button

Comment: Initially this had the effect of returning to the frmCustomer form but always showing Record number 1 instead of the customer for whom the job was added. The reason for this was that the Requery command was used unnecessarily on the After Update event property of the frmJobSheet form. (See systems documentation)

The code was removed and the test worked satisfactorily.

Teacher's signature:

Works Satisfactorily
JR Hartley

Test 25: Print rptArtist report

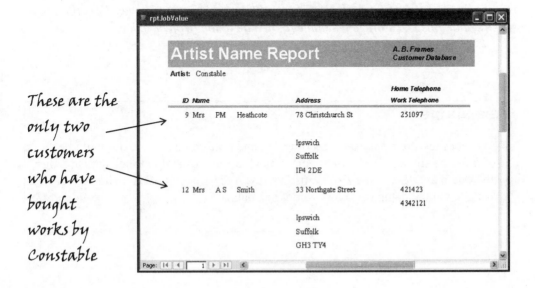

These are the only two customers who have bought works by Constable

Test 29: Mail Merge for Exhibition Customers

This output would look more authentic if it was NOT pasted into a word-processed document. Aim at authenticity rather than neatness in your evidence of testing.

Mrs C A Hallet

St Helens Street

Ipswich

Suffolk FG4 UY7

Dear Mrs Hallet

We have pleasure in inviting you to the Private View of an exhibition of recent East Anglian landscapes in watercolour from the studio of the well known artist **Michael Nolan** at the A. B. Frames Gallery on Thursday 25th November 2004.

Etc etc

Comments on test results can be added by hand. You should also comment on significant test results in the Systems Maintenance section.

Comment: The test allowed the user to create a new letter for exhibition customers, which is automatically stored in the 'My Documents' folder. This is convenient for the end user but for test purposes at school/college had to be changed.

There was no 'village' in the above address and by selecting the option to suppress blank lines in the mail merge dialogue box, no unsightly spaces are left.

(In the project write-up, other tests could be shown as above. For the AQA specification this is a sufficient sample to include in the Project report.)

Assessment

Good set of tests but only samples of tests done need to be shown. It would be useful for the student to identify some typical, erroneous and extreme data together with system and user tests, also items that test Access need not be included e.g. closing down the database. Good set of test data.

Section 4 - System Maintenance

1. System overview

This section should give sufficient information to enable a programmer or someone reasonably expert in the software (Access in this case) to maintain your system

This Customer Information system is designed to keep records of customer profiles and their past orders. It is designed to run alongside the current manual system of recording orders, rather than replacing it. The computer will be in the shop and the owner can use it to check whether a customer who comes in is already on the database, or to check on past orders.

New data will be added to the database at a convenient time, possibly at the end of the week. The procedure that the user will follow is described in the Design section.

2. Tables and Relationships

Tables and relationships were set up as specified in the Design section. An extra table tblItemType was set up to be used as the source for the Item Type list box in the fsubItems subform of frmJobSheet. It has only one field, specifying different types of item such as Framing, Tapestry, etc.

3. Forms

The menu structure was set up as specified in the Design section. Forms were used as follows:

1. AB Main Menu (see user manual for screenshot)

This is specified as the startup form (using Tools, Startup) and loads automatically when the database is opened.

All buttons either opening other forms or reports, or quitting the database, were placed using wizards.

Macros/Modules used:

On Open event uses a custom-made macro named Maximise, which maximises the form.

2.   AB Reports Menu (see User Manual for screenshot)

All buttons placed using wizards. Maximise macro runs on opening form.

3.   Input forms (see User Manual for screenshots)

Draw the readers attention to code given in an appendix.

> **All buttons and many fields have code modules attached. Listings are shown in Appendix 2.**

The frmCustomer form has a combo box (FindIt) displaying customer surnames so that the user can look up the record for any customer. The record source for this box is a query as follows:

There is no need to repeat pseudocode given in the Design section, but you could refer the reader to it.

SELECT DISTINCT [tblCustomer].Surname
FROM [tblCustomer]
WHERE ((([tblCustomer].Surname) Is Not Null))
ORDER BY [tblCustomer].Surname;

When a surname is selected, a macro named FindCustomer is executed to find and display the first record with the selected surname.

4.   MailMergeHelp form (see User Manual for screenshot)

There are no modules attached to this form.

3. Queries

Queries for reports are as listed in the Design section. The other query named **qryCustomerJob** is used as the source for the frmJobSheet form, and combines all the Job sheet fields with the name and address fields for the customer so that these can be displayed on the frmJobSheet form.

4. Reports

These are as described in the User Manual. All reports were created using wizards and then tailored to produce a more appropriate layout.

5. Mail merge letters

A sample letter named *Exhibition letter* was created and placed in the My Documents folder, which is the default folder for Word documents in Windows. The user may choose to save new letters in a different folder.

6. Macros and general modules

All listings are shown in Appendix 2.

Module name: basMisc.

(General Declarations)

Purpose: To declare two global variables used in the frmCustomer form and frmJobSheet forms.

(Function IsOpen)

Purpose: To check whether a form is open. The function uses the Visual Basic SysCmd function, which returns the state of a specified database object to indicate whether the object is open, a new object, or has been changed but not saved.

Module name: Maximise

Purpose: To maximise all forms on opening

7. Discussion of test results

Two extra reports named rptCustomerTestData and rptJobsTestData were generated using wizards to give a hard copy of all test data used during testing. This greatly simplified the process of determining the expected output for many of the tests, and what data to use for new tests when new modules were added. The two reports are printed in Appendix 1.

You can print out the test data that you use directly from Access, either by creating a special report or by printing the tables. Do this regularly as you add new tests, so that you can easily see what output to expect from various queries and reports.

The tests threw up several minor errors which have been corrected. The following points were noted:

♦ if the user enters a JobNo that already exists, he/she is not informed of the error until an attempt is made to leave the form, either to enter the fsubItems subform, delete the record or return to the Customer form. Solution: display a message on leaving the field.

♦ if the user has inadvertently left 0 in the JobNo field and then attempts to return to the frmCustomer form, a Job with ID 0 will be saved the first time. The second time, a 'Duplicate ID' error message will be displayed. The user will have to enter a different ID and then delete the record. Solution: As above; display a message on leaving field ('JobNo must be entered').

♦ If Word is already open when the user starts the Mail Merge from Access, a second version of Word is automatically opened, which could cause 'Out of Memory' problems. Solution: Educate the user to close Word first, or to perform the Mail Merge directly from Word.

The complete system occupied over 7 Mb of hard disk space. In order to transfer it to the user's machine it was zipped onto two floppy disks. The following problems arose on the user's PC:

♦ The screen was an older model, of lower resolution, which meant that some of the text on the forms did not fit on the screen. The forms were adjusted for the user's screen.

♦ The procedure for splitting the database into separate files for Data and Application (using Tools, Add-ins, Database Splitter) resulted in a message 'Not available' so this could not be done. This means that when a backup is done, the application as well as the data has to be backed up. It also means that it is not possible to hold, on the user's machine, a separate file of test data for use in the event of any problems arising.

Assessment

System Maintenance – need to show some evidence in 'design view' of forms, reports, queries etc. (e.g. the relationship diagram needs to be included as it provides evidence that the system has been built).

It is a good idea to include a list of all the elements developed together, including variables used, with their descriptions and cross-reference this to the program code and the 'design views'. (There is no need to include any wizard code – better to write the routine.) Also it is a good idea to use the commenting features of the programming language rather than hand annotation.

Section 5 - User Documentation

See separate section at the end of the project documentation.

Assessment

Lovely user manual but for CPT6 only a sample is required e.g. entering a customer and a job for them together with a report. The manual could do with samples of error messages and error recovery procedures.

Section 6 - Appraisal

Relate your appraisal to the objectives listed in the Analysis section.

The system has been completed and installed on the user's PC. It was completed in the manner originally designed and agreed with the user, and is straightforward to use.

Referring to the original objectives listed in the Analysis section:

Note that the AQA only allocates 5% of the total marks to the Appraisal, whereas other Boards may allocate up to 20% to this section.

1. It takes only a few seconds to establish whether a customer is on file with the 50 or so records on file at the moment.

2. It is easy to go from the frmCustomer form to the frmJobSheet form using a command button, and details are automatically displayed in the Job Sheet.

3. Mrs Daniels had some problems initially with data entry, confusing Jobs and Items, as this aspect works a little differently from the manual system. However she has now entered data for over 100 customers and has no problems to report.

    Particular attention has been paid to default values, tab order, automatic capitalisation of initials and post codes. One problem which has come to light is that only 4 characters were allowed for 'Title', and sometimes Mrs Daniels would like to enter 'Mr and Mrs'. This can easily be adjusted.

4. All jobs for a particular customer are displayed in a subform, so it is a matter of a few seconds to double-click on a particular job to bring up the details. However, the system does not allow the user to easily look up a job from the job number (JobNo); a job can only be located by first looking up the customer, and then double-clicking the job number in the subform. It would be a good idea to add this look-up facility to the frmJobSheet form, and it would be quite simple to add a button to do so.

5. Multi-item jobs are provided for by using a subform in the frmJobSheet form.

6. All reports are implemented as specified.

7. The user has found the mail merge quite complex to perform, and in retrospect it may have been a good idea to set up sample letters to match each data source query, as it would then be possible to automate this aspect of the program more fully. However, some of the problems are more to do with the user's unfamiliarity with the process of changing folders in Windows and remembering where letters have been stored than with weaknesses in the customer database.

8. See 7 above. When Mrs Daniels has completed the data entry of existing customers, I plan to go over with her the steps involved in writing a new letter and performing the mail merge, using her computer.

You should ask the user to write you a letter realistically evaluating the strengths and weaknesses of your system from their point of view. This MUST be authentic to be of any value.

9. The menus work as planned.

Some other minor problems have been noted in the 'Discussion of Test Results' in the Systems Maintenance section.

The AQA mark scheme specifies the inclusion of 'analysis of feedback from users' for full marks in this section.

The next stage in computerisation could very well be to integrate this database with an accounts system, since all orders are stored together with the order values.

Assessment

The evaluation is clearly related to the objectives, but sometimes more detail is required e.g. all reports are implemented as specified does not really relate to the objectives.   E.g. A list of all business customers as provided by the RptBusinessCustomer clearly relates the solution to the original objective. Also clear evidence of user feedback is required and it needs to be analysed by the student who can then identify improvements and how they can be incorporated into the system.

Assessment of Technical Solution

Technical solution – a working project of adequate scope that does what the user wants. However more skills would need to be shown in the coding for a computing student. This could involve the use of SQL as well as VBA. Also perhaps those customers who have not purchased anything recently need archiving.

A.B.Frames

Customer Database

User Manual

User Manual

Table of Contents

Introduction

This Customer Information system is designed to help you with two main tasks:

♦ keep track of all customer jobs so that you can easily look up a past job if required, or find out who your best customers are

♦ keep track of all your customers and their major interests, such as particular artists or subjects, having tapestries framed, etc. so that you can send letters to carefully selected customers informing them of exhibitions, special offers and so on.

The system has been designed in Access 2003 running under Windows XP. You will need a PC with at least 128Mb of memory, and 12Mb of free space on your hard disk to use the system effectively.

Initial Set-up

Passwords

To remove or change the current password required to enter the database, you must choose *Unset Database Password* from the *Tools > Security* menu at the top of the screen. If you then wish to add a new password, go again to the *Tools* menu and the option should now have changed to *Set Database Password*. Select this option, and then type in and verify the new password when asked. **Note: the password is case sensitive, e.g., if the password is "AB", it will not allow access if you type in "ab".**

Menu options

The Main Menu will automatically appear when you open the database.

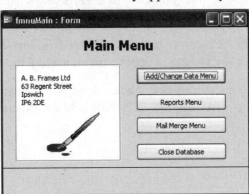

Figure 1: The main menu

Entering Customers and Jobs

Adding a Customer

To enter a new customer you select Customers/Orders from the Main Menu to open the frmCustomer form. Click the *Add Customer* Button, and the *CustomerID* will automatically increment its value. You can then enter all other details.

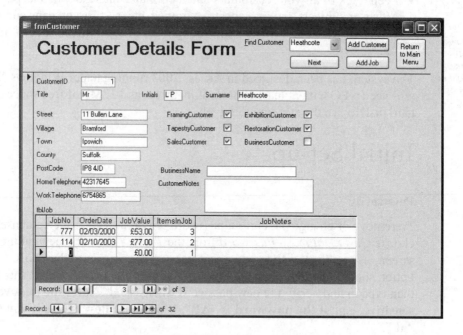

Figure 2: The frmCustomer form

Notes on the frmCustomer Form:

Give the user guidance on data entry where necessary

♦ Ipswich is the default town, and Suffolk the default county but you can of course change these entries.

♦ If you enter Customer Initials or Postcode in lower case letters, they will automatically change to upper case on leaving the field

♦ If you do not specify that the customer is a business customer, when you tab out of the BusinessCustomer (Yes/No) field the BusinessName field will be skipped.

Adding a job

In order to add a job for a customer you must first have that customer's details up on the frmCustomer form (this will already be the case if you have just entered the customer). You can find any customer's record by clicking the arrow in the *Find Customer* box at the top of the form, and selecting the surname of the customer you are looking for. Alternatively you can type in the surname you are looking for in the box. If the details that appear have the correct surname but it is not the correct customer, clicking the *Next* button will take you to the next customer with that surname.

When you have the correct details on screen, select the *Add Job* button. This will take you to the Job Details form, and the CustomerID, name and address should automatically appear in the top right of the form. You can then enter the *Job No* and *Order date*, followed by the rest of the Job Details.

When this is complete, return to the frmCustomer form by clicking the *Return to frmCustomer form* button at the top right of the form. On return to the frmCustomer form you will see that the Job details you have just entered are in the box at the bottom of the form, along with all other previous jobs.

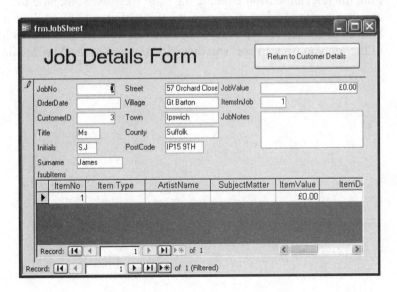

Figure 3: The Job Details form

Notes on the Job Details form

♦ After entering the items, when you tab into the Job Value and Items In Job fields, they will be automatically calculated and displayed.

- You should not leave JobNo as 0, even if you change your mind about entering a new job for this customer. Instead, press Escape, which will make the JobNo field blank, and it will then be safe to exit the form.

Changing Job Details

In order to change details of a job, you must have the relevant customer's details up on the frmCustomer form. Find the job in the box at the bottom of the form, and double-click on the *Job No* of the job you wish to change, and this will take you to the Job Details form.

If you want to delete the job altogether, you can do this in the frmCustomer form by simply highlighting the row which contains the job you wish to delete, and pressing *Delete* on the keyboard.

Looking up Customer Details

Looking up previous jobs for a customer

Find the relevant customer using the *Find Customer* box, and the *Next* button. You can then see the summary of each job the customer has had done in the box at the bottom of the screen. In order to see the full job details, double-click on the *Job No* of the job you want to see, and this will take you to the Job Details form.

Reports

When you select **Reports Menu** from the main menu, a second menu appears:

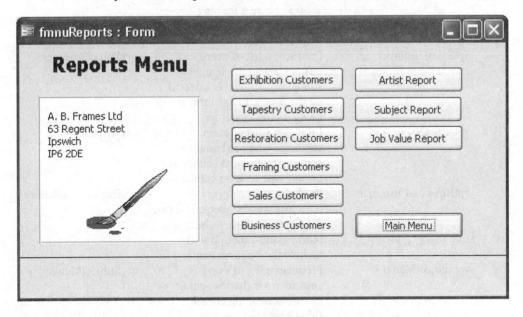

Figure 4: The Reports menu

Summary of Each Report

Report Name	What It Does	Query it is Based on
rptExhibitionCustomer	Produces a list of every customer who has bought something at an exhibition, or is selected on the *frmCustomer* form as being an exhibition customer.	qryExhibitionCustomer
rptTapestryCustomer	Produces a list of every customer who has had a tapestry framed, or who is selected on the *frmCustomer* form as being a tapestry customer	qryTapestryCustomer
rptRestorationCustomer	Produces a list of every customer who has had something restored or who is selected on the *frmCustomer* form as being a restoration customer	qryRestorationCustomer

rptFramingCustomer	Produces a list of every customer who has had something framed, or who is selected on the *frmCustomer* form as being a framing customer	qryFramingCustomer
rptSalesCustomer	Produces a list of every customer who has bought something, or who is selected on the *frmCustomer* form as being a sales customer	qrySalesCustomer
rptArtistName	Produces a list of every customer who has bought a certain artist's work, either as a normal sale or in an exhibition	qryArtistName
rptBusinessCustomer	Produces a list of every customer who is selected on the *frmCustomer* form as being a business customer. It will include the business names	qryBusinessCustomer
rptSubjectMatter	Produces a list of every customer who has bought a picture containing certain subject matter	qrySubjectMatter
rptJobValue	Produces a list of every customer who has spent more than the amount you type in	qryJobValue

Viewing a report on screen

In the Reports menu, click the report you want to view. If the report requires information, a dialogue box will appear asking you to type in a word or value. The report will then appear on screen for you to view. If the report is more than one page long, you can get to the other pages by using the navigation buttons at the bottom of the screen as shown in Figure 5:

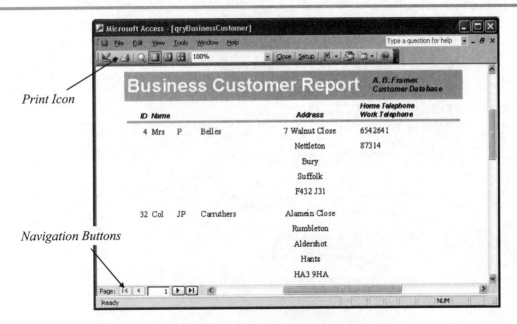

Print Icon

Navigation Buttons

Figure 5: Viewing a report before printing it

Printing a report

To print a report you first view it on screen, then click the print icon at the top of the screen, as shown above.

Mail Merge

For each query that you will want to use as the basis of a mail merge you will need a different merge letter, which you will create yourself as the need arises, and save in the My Documents folder using a meaningful name (e.g. **Sales letter Sep 04.doc** for a letter sent to all Sales customers in September 2004).

To perform a mail merge, you can select the Mail Merge option from the main menu to bring up further instructions, as shown below. Once you get used to the process, you can skip the menu option and open the database window directly.

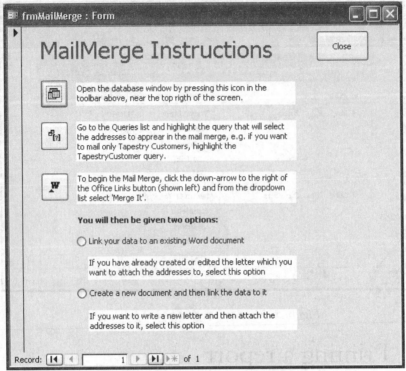

Figure 6: Instructions for the Mail Merge

The steps in the mail merge are as follows:

1. From the database window, click the Queries tab and click qryBusinessCustomer to select it. This will be the source of names and addresses for the mail merge.

OfficeLinks tool

2. Press the down arrow to the right of the OfficeLinks tool. Select Merge it from the pop-up menu.

3. The Microsoft Word Mail Merge Wizard dialogue box opens. If you want to create a new letter, select the second option: Create a new document and then link the data to it.

4. Word opens ready to create the standard letter. Press Enter about 6 times to leave some space at the top of the letter for a standard letterhead, inserting the date, etc.

5. Click the Insert Merge Field in the menu bar. The Insert Merge Field dialogue is displayed.

Figure 7: Inserting merge fields

6.   Double-click Title. The field <<Title>> is placed in your letter. Place the other fields for name and address, leaving spaces and pressing Enter for each new line. The actual text of the letter will be altered by the user. Your letter should appear something like Figure 8.

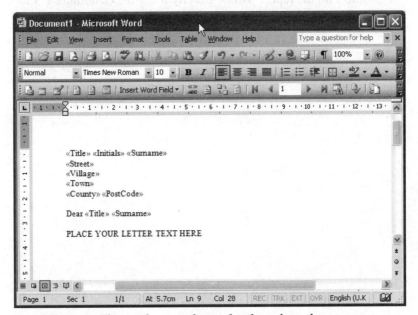

Figure 8: The mail merge letter for the selected customers

7.   Select Tools, Letters and Mailings, Mail Merge and click Step 3: Merge.

8.   In the Mail Merge task pane, go through each of the steps pressing Next (no options need changing for a simple mail merge).

9.   A letter appears for each selected customer, which can be printed.

If you have a merge letter for the query you wish to use, open up that letter so you have it on screen, and make any changes you wish to it, such as changing the date, and the main letter. The merge fields should not need to be changed.

1. Go to Tools, Letters and Mailings, Mail Merge, and work through the steps in order.

2. Go to File, Print, Current Page to check the letters.

3. If the letter is satisfactory, print all the letters by going to File, Print, All.

4. Close the actual merge document without saving. Access will have given it a name such as Form Letters1.

Keeping a record of who was mailed

If you would like to keep a record of who you have mailed, you should print a report straight after you have done the mail merge. For example, if you have mailed all tapestry customers using a merge based on the qryTapestryCustomer query, then go to the reports menu and click Tapestry Customer Report, and then print the report by pressing the print icon as explained earlier. The list of customers on the report will be exactly the same customers as those who are in the mail merge.

Appendix 1

Test Data

ID	Title	Surname	Init	Street	Village	Town	County	PostCode	Home Tel	Work Tel	Sales	Framing	Rest	Tapestry	Exhib	Business	Business Name
1	Mr	Heathcote	LP	11 Bullen Lane	Bramford	Ipswich	Suffolk	IP8 4JD	42317645	6754865	Yes	Yes	Yes	Yes	Yes	No	
2	Mrs	Head	OH	43 MacIntyre Rd		Ipswich	Suffolk	IP9 7HJ	349865		Yes	Yes	No	No	Yes	No	
3	Ms	James	SJ	57 Orchard Close	Gt Barton	Ipswich	Suffolk	IP15 9TH	421421	4532421	No	No	Yes	No	No	Yes	Solos
4	Mrs	Belles	P	7 Walnut Close	Nettleton	Bury	Suffolk	F432 J31	6542641	87314	No	Yes	Yes	No	No	Yes	Davries Ltd
5	Mr	Jaynes	PE	34 Hervey Street		Sudbury	Suffolk	IP8 7HG	67452651	653765	Yes	No	Yes	Yes	No	No	
6	Mrs	Belles	FR	78 The Street	Bramford	Ipswich	Suffolk	1P4 2DE	4311 431214	421210	No	Yes	No	Yes	No	No	
7	Mr	Cladon	RB	16 Chiltern Ave		Ipswich	Suffolk	IP7 4WE			Yes	No	No	No	No	No	
8	Mr	Jenkins	B	15 Upper Terrace		Ipswich	Suffolk	IP3 4AR			Yes	No	No	No	No	No	
9	Mrs	Heathcote	PM	78 Christchurch St		Ipswich	Suffolk	IP4 2DE	251097		Yes	Yes	Yes	No	No	No	
10	Mr	Blair	TW	10 Downing Street		London		SW1A 2AA			Yes	Yes	Yes	Yes	No	No	
11	Mr	Feavyour	JA	29 Hervey Street		Ipswich	Suffolk	ER3 RT5	43432532	3532531	No	Yes	No	No	No	No	
12	Mrs	Smith	AS	33 Northgate Street		Ipswich	Suffolk	GH3 TY4	421423	4342121	Yes	No	No	No	No	No	
13	Mrs	Hallet	CA	St Helens Street		Ipswich	Suffolk	FG4 UY7	4325342	864643	No	No	No	No	Yes	No	
14	Mrs	Cooper	CS	99 Wimble Street		Ealing	London	W12 6RT	543654	876934	No	No	No	Yes	Yes	No	
15	Ms	Thomas	PJ	56 Rosecroft Rd							No	No	No	No	Yes	No	
16	Mr	James	ER	25 Roman Road		Colchester	Essex	CO9 7YH			No	No	No	No	No	No	
17	Mrs	Williams	GH	12 Burlington Rd		Ipswich	Suffolk				No	No	No	No	Yes	No	
18	Mrs	Morgan	CT	10 St Matthews Street		Ipswich	Suffolk				No	No	No	No	No	No	
19	Mrs	Golding	D	13 Bullen Lane	Bramford	Ipswich	Suffolk	IP8 4JD	321642	431531	Yes	Yes	No	No	No	No	
20	Miss	Johns		21 Benacre Road		Ipswich	Suffolk			256571	No	Yes	No	No	No	No	
21	Mrs	Weeden	J	Chalet, Church Rd	Elmswell	Ipswich	Suffolk		264117		No	No	No	No	No	No	
22	Miss	Heathcote	FR	56 Withipoll Street		Ipswich	Suffolk	IP4 3SE	579997		Yes	Yes	Yes	Yes	Yes	No	
23	Mr	Zelter	Z	The White House	Quarry Rd	Orford	Suffolk				Yes	Yes	Yes	Yes	No	No	
24	Mr	Ferdinand	T			Ipswich	Suffolk				No	Yes	No	No	No	No	
25	Mr	Honeycut	BJ	Back Road	Great Weasel	Porking	Suffolk	IP4 5FG			No	Yes	No	No	No	No	
26	Mr	Pierce	HK	13 High St	Little Snoring		Suffolk	IP7 2NM			No	No	Yes	Yes	No	Yes	
27	Mrs	Donohue	K	Wisteria Rise	Candleford		Suffolk	IP9 5GH			No	No	No	No	No	Yes	
28	Ms	Jones	B	Hill House	Main St	Wuthering	Norfolk	NN6 8DF			No	No	No	No	Yes	No	
29	Mr	Colquhoun	L	Shenanigan		Dublin	Eire				No	No	No	No	No	No	
30	Cmdr	Chumley	S	Moby Dock		Shotley	Suffolk	IP7 3KK			Yes	No	No	No	No	No	
31	Mr	Honeycut	WW	Tide Mill	Lower Snoring	Woodbridge	Suffolk	IP23 6NM			No	No	Yes	Yes	No	Yes	
32	Col	Carruthers	JP	Alamein Close	Rumbleton	Aldershot	Hants	HA3 9HA			No	Yes	Yes	Yes	No	Yes	

JobNo	ItemNo	ItemType	ArtistName	SubjectMatter	ItemValue	Cust. ID	OrderDate
4	1	Sales	Constable	landscape	£150.00	9	23/05/2003
5	1	Sales	Constable	landscape	£200.00	12	24/05/2003
17	1	Framing			£50.00	2	13/06/2003
17	2	Sales	Dali	abstract	£75.00	2	13/06/2003
31	1	Restoration			£5.00	23	14/06/2003
33	1	Framing			£5.00	23	15/06/2003
34	1	Tapestry			£5.00	23	16/06/2003
35	1	Exhibition			£5.00	23	17/06/2003
36	1	Sales	Jerry Jenkins	flowers	£5.00	23	18/06/2003
43	1	Framing			£17.00	24	01/09/2003
45	1	Sales	Lowry	matchstick men	£23.00	5	01/02/2003
76	1	Sales	Bill Smith	still life	£44.00	7	02/03/2003
76	2	Sales	Bill Smith	still life	£3.00	7	02/03/2003
114	1	Sales	Ted Hunter	cats	£27.00	1	02/10/2003
114	2	Sales	Ted Hunter	cats	£50.00	1	02/10/2003
123	1	Sales	Turner	landscape	£73.00	5	02/02/2003
155	1	Framing	Bates	horses	£25.00	11	01/11/2003
299	1	Restoration			£55.00	4	03/06/2003
299	2	Sales	Lowry	matchstick men	£60.00	4	03/06/2003
599	1	Framing			£23.00	1	03/06/2003
599	2	Sales	Van Gough	portrait	£7.00	1	03/06/2003
677	1	Sales	Mondrian	cubes	£11.00	1	01/01/2003
777	1	Framing			£33.00	1	02/03/2004
777	2	Sales	Andrew Foster	flowers	£20.00	1	02/03/2004
777	3	Sales	Mondrian	cubes	£0.00	1	02/03/2004
778	1	Sales	Andrew Foster	dogs	£50.00	22	03/05/2003
778	2	Framing		cats	£20.00	22	03/05/2003
911	1	Sales	James Harvey	dogs	£50.00	12	09/07/2003
3337	1	Sales	Van Gough	flowers	£35.00	10	03/09/2003
3337	2	Framing			£25.00	10	03/09/2003
3337	3	Restoration			£5.00	10	03/09/2003
3337	4	Sales	A Painter	dogs	£5.00	10	03/09/2003
3337	5	Restoration			£10.00	10	03/09/2003
5098	1	Framing			£20.10	21	01/09/2002
5099	1	Framing			£48.00	20	05/09/2002
5656	1	Sales	Andrew Foster	dogs	£60.00	19	05/07/2003
5656	2	Framing			£40.00	19	05/07/2003
6000	1	Exhibition			£3,000.00	1	22/08/2004
6001	1	Exhibition			£2,225.00	2	22/08/2004

Appendix 2
Module Listings

1. Global Module

Name: **basMisc**

Purpose: **To declare global variables**

To define global function IsOpen

```
Option Compare Database
        Public DisplayJob As Boolean
        Public JobNum As Long
Option Explicit
```

used in frmJobSheet and fsubItem subform

Annotate your listings by hand. Make clear which modules YOU wrote, and which code was created automatically by wizards.

```
Public Function IsOpen(ByVal StrFormName As String) As Boolean
' Returns True if the specified form is open in form view

Const conDesignView = 0
Const conObjStateClosed = 0
IsOpen = False
If SysCmd(acSysCmdGetObjectState, acForm, StrFormName) <> conObjStateClosed Then
    If Forms(StrFormName).CurrentView <> conDesignView Then
        IsOpen = True
    End If
End If

End Function
```

SysCmd is a built-in Visual Basic function

2. frmCustomer form (see User Manual for screenshot)

All buttons and many fields have code modules attached. Listings are shown below.

```
Option Compare Database
Option Explicit

Private Sub BusinessCustomer_Exit(Cancel As Integer)
    'Skip the Business Name control if not a business customer
    If BusinessCustomer = True Then
        BusinessName.SetFocus
    Else
        CustomerNotes.SetFocus
    End If
End Sub
```

```
Private Sub Find_Next_Click()
    'This module runs when the Find Next button is presssed.
    'It finds the next customer with the same surname as the current record.
    'If there are no more matching customers, the button caption changes to 'No More'

    Dim CR As String

    CR = CustomerID
    Surname.SetFocus
    DoCmd.FindRecord (Surname), , , , , , False
    FindNext.SetFocus

    If CustomerID = CR Then
        FindNext.Caption = "No more"
    End If
End Sub
```

Must set the parameter to False otherwise it gets stuck on current record

```
Private Sub Find_Next_LostFocus()
    FindNext.Caption = "Next"
End Sub


Private Sub Form_Current()
    'This ensures that the surname in the combo box matches the current record
    FindIt = Surname
End Sub


Sub AddCustomer_Click()
    'This module runs when the Add Customer button is clicked

    Dim CustID As Long                          'variable type Long Integer
    On Error GoTo Err_AddCustomer_Click         'built-in error routine

    DoCmd.GoToRecord , , acLast
    CustID = CustomerID                         'save the value of CustomerID
    If CustID = 0 Then                          'allow for the very first record
        CustomerID = 1
    Else
        DoCmd.GoToRecord , , acNext             'go to a new record
        CustomerID = CustID + 1                 'increment the CustomerID
    End If
    Title.SetFocus                              'move cursor to Title control

Exit_AddCustomer_Click:
    Exit Sub


Err_AddCustomer_Click:
    MsgBox Err.Description
    Resume Exit_AddCustomer_Cl

End Sub
```

This module automatically assigns the next number to a new customer

```
Private Sub Initials_Exit(Cancel As Integer)
    'Change Initials to uppercase
    Initials = UCase(Initials)
End Sub


Private Sub Postcode_Exit(Cancel As Integer)
    'Change Post Code to uppercase
    Postcode = UCase(Postcode)
End Sub


Sub AddJob_Click()
On Error GoTo Err_AddJob_Click
    'Clicking the Add Job button causes this module to be run

    Dim stDocName As String
    Dim stLinkCriteria As String

    'The form must be refreshed before opening the Job sheet
    'in order to save the customer record
    Me.Refresh

    If IsNull(Me![Surname]) Then
        MsgBox "Enter customer information before entering job"
    Else
        'DisplayJob is a global variable defined in basMisc
        'and tested in frmJobSheet On Open to determine what
        'event opened the frmJobSheet form, pressing the Add Job button
        'or double-clicking a JobNo in the subform.

        DisplayJob = False
        stDocName = "frmJobSheet"

        stLinkCriteria = "[CustomerID]=" & Me![CustomerID]
        DoCmd.OpenForm stDocName, , , stLinkCriteria
    End If

Exit_AddJob_Click:
    Exit Sub

Err_AddJob_Click:
    MsgBox Err.Description
    Resume Exit_AddJob_Click

End Sub
```

This code is created automatically by the wizard when you place a command to open a form

```
Sub Menu_Click()
'This runs when the Return to Main Menu button is clicked
On Error GoTo Err_Menu_Click

    Dim stDocName As String
    Dim stLinkCriteria As String

    stDocName = "AB Main Menu"
    DoCmd.OpenForm stDocName, , , stLinkCriteria

Exit_Menu_Click:
    Exit Sub

Err_Menu_Click:
    MsgBox Err.Description
    Resume Exit_Menu_Click

End Sub
```

Command button code created automatically by wizard

3.   fsubJobs (Subform)

This subform of the customer form displays a summary of all the previous jobs for the current customer. Details of any job can be obtained by double-clicking a JobNo.

The Double-click event module is shown below.

```
Private Sub JobNO_DblClick(Cancel As Integer)
    'DisplayJob and JobNum are public variables declared in the module Misc.
    'DisplayJob is  is set to TRUE here
    'to indicate that the user has double-clicked JobNo.
    'It will be tested in the Open event of the Job Sheet form.
    'JobNum will also be used in the Open event of the Job Sheet form.
    'to enable the correct Job Sheet to be found and displayed.

    DisplayJob = True
    JobNum = JobNo  ◄───────
    DoCmd.OpenForm "frmJobSheet"
End Sub
```

Current job number saved in JobNum

4.   Job Sheet (see user manual for screenshot)

The Job sheet is opened directly from the frmCustomer form. Modules attached to various events are shown below:

```
Private Sub Form_AfterUpdate()
   If IsOpen("frmCustomer") Then
   ' Requery the subform in the frmCustomer form to show new job
   '      Forms![frmCustomer].Requery

   'Note: Testing showed that this code was not necessary and caused
   'the customer form to open at the first record instead of the current record.

   Else
      MsgBox "Customer Form not open"
   End If
End Sub
```

Function IsOpen is defined in global module basMisc

```
Private Sub Form_Open(Cancel As Integer)
   If IsOpen("frmCustomer") Then
      'DisplayJob is set to TRUE in the fsubJobs (Subform) of the frmCustomer form
      'when a user double-clicks JobNo.
      'DisplayJob is set to FALSE if the user clicks the AddJob button.
      If DisplayJob = False Then
         DoCmd.GoToRecord , , acLast
         If Not IsNull(Me![JobNo]) Then
            DoCmd.GoToRecord , , acNext
         End If
         Forms![frmJobSheet]![CustomerID] = Forms![frmCustomer]![CustomerID]
      Else
         'user wants to display a job whose number was stored in JobNum
         'in the Double-click event code in fsubJobs
         'so look for that job and display it

         JobNo.SetFocus
         DoCmd.FindRecord jobNum
      End If
   Else
      MsgBox "The Customer Details form must be open before you can enter a job"
      DoCmd.Close acForm, "frmJobSheet"
   End If
End Sub
```

```
Private Sub ItemsInJob_Enter()
    Forms![frmJobSheet]![ItemsInJob] = DCount("[ItemNo]", "tblItem",
"[JobNo]=Forms![frmJobSheet].[JobNo]")
End Sub

Private Sub JobValue_Enter()
Forms![frmJobSheet]![JobValue] = DSum("[ItemValue]", "tblItem",
"[JobNo]=Forms![frmJobSheet].[JobNo]")
End Sub


Sub ReturnToCustomer_Click()
On Error GoTo Err_ReturnToCustomer_Click

    'refresh the frmCustomer form so that it displays
    'the changes made in this form
    Forms![frmCustomer].Refresh

    DoCmd.Close
Exit_ReturnToCustomer_Click:
    Exit Sub

Err_ReturnToCustomer_Click:
    MsgBox Err.Description
    Resume Exit_ReturnToCustomer_Click

End Sub
```

These lines were added to the code generated automatically by the command button wizard

5.   fsubItems

This subform allows the user to enter several items on one job sheet. Code for the Item Type exit event module is shown below.

```
Private Sub ItemType_Exit(Cancel As Integer)

'Sets the relevant field in the tblCustomer table according to ItemType

    If IsOpen("frmCustomer") Then
       Select Case Me![ItemType]
          Case "Exhibition"
             Forms![frmCustomer]![ExhibitionCustomer] = True
          Case "Framing"
             Forms![frmCustomer]![FramingCustomer] = True
          Case "Restoration"
             Forms![frmCustomer]![RestorationCustomer] = True
          Case "Sales"
             Forms![frmCustomer]![SalesCustomer] = True
          Case "Tapestry"
             Forms![frmCustomer]![TapestryCustomer] = True
       End Select
    Else
       MsgBox "The Customer form must be open "
    End If
End Sub
```

Index

PROJECT TITLE: **DEVELOPED BY:**

TABLE NAME:

Attribute name	Data type	Length	Default value	Description, validation, comments

Test No.	Test data	Purpose	Expected result	Comment/ Verified